NOT MY SHAME

HEALING CHILDHOOD TRAUMA

DANIELA TILBROOK

CONTENTS

FOREWORD / AUTHOR'S NOTE   v

PART I
THE DARK

1. The Phone Box   3
2. Living with Fear and Faith   8
3. A Hymn, a Belt and the Faraway Tree   14
4. The Wedding and the Shame that Followed   20
5. Survival Tactics and Teenage Years   23
6. University and The Escape Into Alcohol   29
7. Bullying at Work and the Breakdown   32
8. The Memories Return   38
9. Healing Steps   45
10. The Crash That Shook Me Awake   49
11. The Price of Silence   57
12. The Letter   64
13. Meeting In Tisno   70
14. Building a New Life   74
15. Smoke after Fire   79
16. Lockdown and the Death Plan's Fatal Flaw   84
17. The Courtroom Scene   90
18. Not Our Shame   99
19. The Weight of What Wasn't Said   103
20. Hope, Fantasy and the Truth   107
21. Choosing Myself   112
22. Victim Blaming and Disclosure   118
23. The Question That Cut Deep   125

PART II
THE LIGHT

24. Stepping Out of the Dark — 133
25. My Internal Family (IFS) — 144
26. The Attachments That Shape Us — 152
27. Understanding Trauma and Post-Traumatic Growth — 159
28. Understanding the Nervous System – Why Trauma Lives in the Body — 166
29. Understanding Your Daily D.O.S.E — 173
30. Becoming My Own Best Friend, Parent and Healer — 182
31. A Journey into the Unknown—My Ayahuasca Experience — 190
32. When the Soul Speaks — 207
33. LIGHT : The Path to Healing — 212
34. Meeting Our Shadow: The Path to Wholeness — 223
35. Becoming Light — 229

APPENDIX — 235

FOREWORD / AUTHOR'S NOTE

The whisper began 20 years ago: "Why don't you write a book?"

Back then, my world had shattered. I had fought a losing battle against workplace bullying. I wanted to write a book about workplace bullying, but I never finished it. The voice came in: *Who are you to write a book? Who would even listen?*

So I silenced myself before I could finish.

Trauma recovery doesn't move in a straight line—it loops, spirals and shifts in unexpected ways.

The first part of the book—*the dark*—is my personal story.

Part two, *the light*, explores healing, growth and coming to terms with my past.

- Breaking the silence—finding my voice after years of secrecy.

- Self-worth & survival—how early wounds shaped my choices.
- Justice & healing—the long road to confronting the past.

This is more than a personal story; it's a mission to break the stigma of childhood abuse and show that healing is possible. Wherever you are on your journey, I hope this book reminds you: **You are not alone.**

I encourage you to complete the journal prompts included in the second part of this book. While I myself have often skipped over exercises when reading, I've learned that taking the time to do them can be incredibly helpful for personal growth, understanding and healing.

Beyond survival lies reclamation—of voice, self and hope. My journey revealed a critical truth: we are not defined by our wounds, but by the courage it takes to heal them.

Dear Reader,

Before you begin, a gentle heads-up: this book shares deeply personal experiences of childhood trauma and healing. Some passages may stir strong emotions. If it ever feels like too much, please pause. Breathe. Return when you're ready. Your pace matters and your well-being comes first. You deserve care and compassion.

If you have ever felt invisible, ashamed or unworthy, I want you to know this: **You are not alone.**

For years, I carried a secret that felt too heavy to hold, yet too dangerous to put down. I believed that silence would keep me safe; that if I never spoke the words aloud, I could somehow outrun the truth. But shame thrives in the dark, and no matter how fast we run, it follows—until we turn around and face it.

I know how it feels to question your own reality, to wonder if it was really that bad, to downplay your pain because others have "had it worse" I know the weight of self-blame, the exhaustion of keeping the peace at your own expense and the endless loop of *what-ifs* and *if-onlys*.

But here's a truth I wish someone had told me sooner: **What happened to you was not your fault. It was *never* your fault.**

Maybe you've carried this secret for years, or maybe you only just found the words. Maybe you've told someone and been met with disbelief or silence. Maybe you've been gaslit, shamed, or told to "just move on". Maybe you're still trying to figure out where to place all the pain. Wherever you are in your journey, I see you. And I believe you.

Healing is not a straight line. Some days, it will feel

impossible. Others, you will feel like you're drowning in grief, anger and exhaustion. But then there will be moments —small at first—where light starts to break through. A deep breath that feels like a victory. A boundary you never thought you could set. A day when you realise the shame isn't yours to carry anymore.

If you take nothing else from this book, please take this: **You deserve to heal. You deserve peace. You deserve love.**

There is no timeline for healing. There is no "right" way to move forward. Start where you are. Be gentle with yourself. Speak to your inner child with kindness. Find the people who make you feel safe and let them in. And if you haven't found them yet, keep going. There are people out there who will understand, who will listen, who will hold space for you. I promise.

You are not alone.

You are not broken.

And this was never your shame to carry.

With all my love and solidarity,

Daniela

Acknowledgments

> *"Until one is committed, there is hesitancy, the chance to draw back—always ineffectiveness.*
>
> *Concerning all acts of initiative (and creation), there is one elementary truth the ignorance of which kills countless ideas and splendid plans:*
>
> *that the moment one definitely commits oneself, then Providence moves too."*
>
> —W.H. Murray

The moment I fully committed to this book, something shifted. Providence stepped in. Helping hands appeared. Doors opened I hadn't even knocked upon. And I was no longer doing it alone.

To Marcus Young, my incredible book coach and soul brother—this book would not exist without you. You walked beside me through every step of this journey, holding the vision even when I lost sight of it. You gave countless hours, energy, insight and heart to help me craft, refine and bring this story to life. When I doubted myself, when the path felt impossible, you never faltered. Your belief in me never wavered. This book is as much yours as it is mine. I am endlessly grateful.

To Simon Shields, my soul brother who held the light that led me out of shame. You've walked through your own fire and still showed up for me—again and again. A chance meeting in a yoga class became one of the most meaningful friendships of my life. Thank you for being a steady presence, a beta reader, a proofreader and a friend I cherish deeply. I can't wait to read your book one day.

To Anthony Smith, my soul brother across the pond—your courage gave me permission to speak. The way you've alchemised your own trauma has been a guiding light for me. Thank you for showing me what's possible.

To Heroic Public Benefit Corporation—the Coach programme changed my life. After years of being a librarian of the mind, collecting self-help tools but struggling to act, Heroic gave me the structure, courage and clarity to move from theory into practice.

To Brian Johnson—thank you for the honour of being personally coached by you. Thank you for answering the call so others like me could find the courage to answer our own.

To all my friends in the Heroic community—thank you for cheering me on, for sharing your light and for reminding me that I am not alone. We are all here to serve something greater.

To Patricia and Eloy—thank you for listening to early drafts with such patience and encouragement and for being champions of this work from the very beginning.

To my wonderful editor, Samantha Sendor—thank you for coming in at the eleventh hour and editing this book with such care and professionalism. Your work has made a real difference and the readers will feel it.

To my soul sister Lily Royal, our personal development trips together have been so much fun. You are a wonderful travel companion. Thank your for your support and love.

To my soul sister River—thank you for guiding me and

holding my hand from afar. I have always felt your loving presence with me.

To Jonathan Wells—thank you for reading the vulnerable early drafts I was afraid to share and for being one of my first beta readers. Your encouragement meant more than you know.

To all my generous beta readers—thank you for taking the time to engage with the manuscript and offer your insights:

Bob Vanstan, Marc Turczanski, Wendy Moore, Briony Gunson, Amanda Dolton, Jessica Boland—your feedback helped shape this final version.

To Eliza, another thoughtful beta reader and the talented designer behind my book cover—thank you for capturing the heart of this work so beautifully.

To Tom Furnell—thank you for your accountability, companionship and shared writing sessions in the library that helped me build a consistent writing practice.

To Kevin Godding, and to *Coffee in the Wood*—thank you for the warmth of early morning cappuccinos and the quiet encouragement that met me at my 6 a.m. writing sessions. You helped turn lonely writing hours into something between therapy and frothy, caffeine-fuelled delusion.

To my beautiful friend Christine O'Connell, also from across the pond—our conversations helped me find clarity and a deeper sense of purpose.

It truly takes a village to write a book. If your name isn't listed but your support carried me in any way—thank you from the bottom of my heart.

And finally, to my wonderful husband—the unsung hero

in my story. Your love, patience and unwavering support have rewritten the second half of my life into something rich with joy, safety and blessing. You are my rock and I love you so much.

PART I
THE DARK

1
THE PHONE BOX

The glass walls of the phone box were smeared with fingerprints and colourful graffiti. Outside, the world carried on—cars whooshing past, children laughing in the distance—but from within this dim, red booth, time felt frozen.

The sticker was right in front of me, peeling slightly at the edges. 0800 1111.

Childline.

I traced the numbers with my finger, then pressed them into the grimy metal buttons. Each click echoed in the silence.

The line rang once. Twice.

Then a voice. Soft. Kind.

"Hello, you've reached Childline. How can I help?"

My throat tightened. I gripped the cold metal of the receiver harder, my sweaty palm slipping against it. *Just say it. Just say it. If I say it, does that make it real?*

The words wouldn't come.

I squeezed my eyes shut, the walls of the phone box closing in like a cage. My heart pounded so loudly, I was sure she could hear it.

"Hello? Is anyone there?"

I swallowed, my tongue heavy, my lips dry. If I spoke the words–if I let them out–what would happen? Would my whole world shatter? Would they take me away? Would I be believed?

A gust of wind rattled the door. Panic surged through me —what if someone saw me? What if they told Him?

From that day on, even his name felt too dangerous to speak; I could only think of him as Him—a single, towering word that held all his power.

I slammed the receiver down, the clatter echoing in the small space. My breath came in short, sharp bursts as I stared at the phone, my reflection barely visible in the scratched glass that read *"Ozzie was here."*

I tried to speak. But I had failed.

I pushed the door open, stepping back into the warm afternoon air. The world outside was exactly as I had left it— cars still rushing past, people still laughing.

As if nothing had happened.

As if I hadn't just trapped myself in my silence for years to come. I was 13 years old. My nightmare wasn't going to end anytime soon.

I walked home, head down, scuffing the toes of my shoes against the pavement. Church bells rang in the distance; a familiar sound, steady and unshakeable. Mass would be starting soon. My mother would already be there, dressed neatly, hands folded in quiet devotion. My father would be playing the organ.

In our home, faith wasn't just a belief—it was the foundation of everything. The walls were lined with crucifixes and above the dining table hung a picture of Jesus with his disciples. We prayed before meals, before bed, we prayed at Mass. There was a right way to behave, a right way to think, a right way to be.

I had learnt from an early age that certain things were never to be spoken about. Not in the confessional, not in whispered prayers, not even in the dead of night. God saw everything, but some sins were mine alone to bear.

To the outside world, we were the quintessential Croatian Catholic family. My father would deliver the first reading at Mass and play the organ. My mother hosted the priests for dinner. I knew when to smile, when to nod, when to lower my eyes in obedience.

But behind the hymns and the scripture, there were things I could not reconcile. *If we were so devoted, why did I feel so ashamed? If God was watching over us, why wasn't He stopping it?*

I never dared to ask.

And even if I had, who would have listened?

That night, we sat for dinner as a family. My mother was a fantastic cook, always making yummy food. After dinner, she cleared plates while my father switched on the news. Nothing seemed out of place. Nothing, except the weird feeling in my belly that hadn't left since the moment I hung up the phone.

I told myself I was safe. *Maybe tonight would be different.*

Maybe the phone call had changed something, even though I hadn't uttered a word.

The only sound to be heard was the low hum of the television in the living room; a sound that only emphasised the silence. I had already brushed my teeth and slipped under my cosy duvet. My body was tired, but my mind was awake–alert, waiting.

The floorboards creaked from outside my bedroom door.

My whole body tensed under the duvet. I kept my breathing slow and steady—pretending to be asleep had worked before. *Maybe it would work again tonight.*

The door handle turned. A shadow stretched across my bedroom floor.

I squeezed my eyes tighter, willing myself invisible.

Maybe tonight would be different.

But deep down, I already knew it wouldn't be.

THE SILENCE BEGINS

I was seven years old when I learnt that silence was safer.

He was *Tata*—the Croatian word for Dad—the man who tucked me in at night, taught me to swim and played the organ at church on Sundays.

My father. My protector. The man I was supposed to trust. I had no reason to doubt Him—until I did.

He had once been a Catholic priest. People whispered about it, but no one dared to question it. He left the priesthood and later married my mother. My childhood would teach me that monsters don't always hide in the shadows.

Sometimes, they stand in the light, cloaked in the language of faith and family, smiling as they preach about sin whilst committing the worst at home.

2

LIVING WITH FEAR AND FAITH

The next morning his sharp voice shattered my sleep.

"U Školu!" —*To school*. The words cut through my dreams, yanking me back to reality. It was never a gentle wake-up.

We were a Croatian family living in London and Croatian was the language spoken in our home. Speaking English in the house was frowned upon, although my brothers and I often did—it was simply easier for us.

Don't get me wrong—I loved school. I felt safe there. But the morning cry was never a pleasant way to start the day.

I rolled onto my side, my cosy duvet still enveloping my body, as I willed myself to move. Downstairs, my mother hummed softly as she clattered dishes in the sink. The morning news mumbled in the background. Everything looked the way it always did.

I pulled on my school uniform, tied back my hair and

grabbed my bag. If I walked quickly, I'd have time to get to school early and finish my homework. I was always telling myself that I'd do it the night before, but somehow, that never seemed to happen.

Still, it wasn't just homework that made me eager to leave the house; I had reading to look forward to. If I finished my work fast enough, I could squeeze in a few pages of *Third Year at Malory Towers*. I loved books and was working my way through everything Enid Blyton had ever written.

And then there was sport. I wasn't the best at schoolwork, but out on the playground, I felt truly free. We'd play British Bulldog, running and dodging with breathless laughter as our shrieks echoed in the thrill of the chase, wiping everything else from my mind.

At school, I could breathe.

Most of the time.

"Pay attention, Daniela!" snapped Sister Catherine, rapping her ruler against the desk.

I could feel my cheeks turn crimson as the class turned to look at me. I had been staring out of the window, watching the leaves flutter in the wind.

I had not really been present. At least not fully. I was still in the phone box, the receiver cold in my hands, the voice on the other end waiting for me to speak.

"Sorry, Sister Catherine," I muttered, dropping my gaze.

I forced myself to focus, to sit up straight, to *look* like I was paying attention. *Be good. Don't get in trouble. Stay invisible.*

The lesson dragged on, numbers and letters swimming on the blackboard. As the bell rang, I reached for my bag and rushed out of the classroom—and then it happened.

My glasses slipped from my face, fell on the floor and broke.

For a moment, I just stared. One lens had popped out, a long fracture splitting the other in two. My glasses were now useless. I would need new ones.

The room blurred around me. My breath came too fast, too sharp. *Oh God. Oh God. Oh God.*

I was crying before I even realised it.

A hand touched my shoulder.

"Daniela?" It was Sister Catherine. "It's alright, we'll get them fixed. Don't worry."

But I couldn't stop shaking.

She didn't understand. It wasn't about the glasses; it was about what would happen when I got home.

I had ruined something. I had been careless. I had done something *wrong*.

I gulped back sobs, my fingers gripping the broken frames. *I... I didn't mean to.*

Sister Catherine crouched beside me.

"Shhh, it's okay. We'll tell your parents. They'll understand."

I wanted to tell her. I wanted to scream that she was wrong. *Mistakes at home were not tolerated. Even a small spill of something would get an overreaction. Broken glasses were considered a serious offence. My parents were going to kill me.*

I didn't say anything. Instead, I nodded.

She sighed and patted my hand, then pulled a notepad from her desk and began to write a letter for me to take home to my parents. I could already see that letter in my mother's hands. Her lips pressed together. The way she would hold it with a disapproving look.

Sister Catherine handed me the sealed envelope.

"Give this to your parents when you get home."

I nodded again, my stomach butterflies were back. *I would rather have disappeared than hand them that letter.*

I clutched the letter in one hand and my broken glasses in the other as I stepped through the school gates.

Other kids ran ahead, laughing, carefree. They didn't have to worry about what waited for them at home. They weren't holding a letter that felt heavier than a sack of potatoes. Even better, they could actually see where they were going.

I blinked, trying to focus on the pavement beneath me. I was practically blind without my glasses. I could make out the outlines of houses and people, but their faces and their expressions were just smudges of light and shadow.

I hated those stupid glasses.

I had hated them since the day I got them. Pink National Health glasses that made me look like a geek. Kids at school called me "four eyes" and sometimes I would take them off, just for a little while, just to feel *normal*.

But then the world would disappear.

At least when I was wearing them, I could pretend I wasn't lost.

Now, with one lens cracked and the other missing, I felt more lost than ever.

I walked slower than usual, dragging my feet. I knew every crack in the pavement, every loose stone on the path. If

I took small steps, if I delayed just a little longer, maybe time would stretch out and I'd never have to reach my front door.

The letter was in my hand.

I could feel the tightness in my throat, the heat pressing from behind my eyes. I forced myself not to cry. Crying wouldn't change anything.

My street came into view. My house. The front door.

I took a breath, held it.

And then I stepped inside.

As soon as I crossed the threshold, I could hear her in the kitchen and the dishes clattering against the sink basin. My mum was making *juha*—Croatian for soup.

She didn't look up. "Where have you been?"

I hesitated, still gripping the letter tightly in my hand. I wanted to hold onto it a little longer, to delay what was coming, but there was no point. She'd see the glasses eventually.

I placed the note on the kitchen table.

"Sister Catherine said to give you this."

That's when she turned.

Her eyes flicked to the letter, then to my face. And then she saw the glasses. The crack running through the lens, the way I was holding them together like I could somehow undo what had happened.

Her mouth visibly tightened as she pursed her lips.

"*Guska!*" Goose. Followed by, "Stupid."

It was sharp, cutting—the name she used when I had done something wrong.

I flinched, my fingers tightening around the broken frames.

She took the letter and read it. I watched her eyes scan the words, her lips pressing together in that way that always made my stomach twist.

The air felt too still.

Then, something in the energy had shifted. Her shoulders dropped slightly. The hardness in her expression loosened.

She exhaled through her mouth, shaking her head.

"You are so clumsy."

It wasn't kindness exactly, but it wasn't the sharp bite I was expecting.

For a moment, I thought she might say something else—something worse, or maybe something better. But instead, my mum just folded the letter neatly and placed it aside.

"Go get changed out of your uniform," she said, turning back to the sink.

The conversation was over.

I stood there for a second longer, waiting. For what, I wasn't sure. It was clear I had been dismissed.

Then I walked to my room and changed out of my uniform, making sure I folded it neatly and placed it on the chair like I was supposed to.

Then I pulled *Third Year at Malory Towers* from my bag and flipped to the page where I'd left off.

I wasn't in my bedroom anymore. I was at Malory Towers, by the sea, with girls who had real friendships and exciting adventures.

I could pretend, just for a little while, that I was there with them too.

3

A HYMN, A BELT AND THE FARAWAY TREE

I didn't steal it. Not really. I just wanted to learn the words.

The hymn book sat on my bed, open to the page with *Here I Am, Lord,* its familiar words dancing across the paper.

I loved singing. At Mass, I would listen to the soaring voices around me, wishing I knew all the words by heart. So when I saw the book left unattended at church, I slipped it under my jumper.

I knew what I was doing was wrong. *Thou shalt not steal* is one of the Ten Commandments, after all. But in my seven-year-old heart, it didn't feel like stealing—it felt like borrowing. I told myself I would return the hymn book once I had memorised the words.

But I never did get the chance to return it.

When they found it in my room, the shame came first.

Then the fear. My stomach dropped as my father's voice filled the air—sharp and accusing. My mother's disapproving glare cast over me.

She stood in the doorway, arms folded, eyes narrowed. Then she turned and walked away.

Maybe she didn't want to see what was about to happen. Maybe she couldn't.

My father entered the room and picked up the hymn book from the bed. He held it in his hand, gripping it tightly as He looked at me.

"Stealing is wrong," He said, his voice calm but firm. There was no shouting, no rage—just cold disapproval.

Then He set the book down, took off his belt and began.

The blows came fast and deliberate.

I flinched with each strike, the sting lighting up my skin, the sound louder than the hymns I had once loved.

I bit my lip to stop myself from crying out, knowing that tears would only make it worse.

I hadn't taken it out of greed. I had taken it because I loved it. Because I wanted to sing.

But that didn't matter. In our house, there was no room for mistakes. No space for understanding. No one asked why.

I was stupid. I was clumsy. I was Guska. A fool. Stupid. Clumsy. Guska. A fool. And now... a thief.

Even though I understood that stealing wasn't right, I also knew deep down that the punishment didn't fit the crime.

When it was over, my skin stung and my hands trembled, but the ache in my chest was worse.

It wasn't just the pain—it was the feeling that love, in this house, had conditions. That wanting something—even something as small as a hymn book—could bring punishment.

So I learned. Learned to want less.

Learned to take up less space.

Learned that invisibility could serve me well.

But safety was an illusion.

The Beginnings of Abuse

It started with bedtime stories. His voice, deep and steady, reading about princesses, dragons and faraway lands.

I liked the way his words fell over me as I closed my eyes. How they lifted me out of the room, away from the creeping unease in my belly.

Until the stories stopped. And the *touch* began.

His hand slid beneath the covers. At first, just resting there, as if it belonged. My body stiffened, but I didn't move. I held my breath, waiting, hoping He would stop.

He didn't.

His fingers found places they should never go, his voice still smooth, still steady, as if nothing had changed. As if this was just another part of the bedtime routine.

That sick feeling in my tummy came back, stronger this time—a heavy twist that made me feel like I might throw up. I didn't understand what was happening, but something inside me whispered that it was wrong. That this wasn't how stories were meant to end.

I kept my eyes shut, pretending I was somewhere else.

If I didn't move, if I stayed quiet, maybe I could disappear.

I don't recall when I started dissociating, but I do remember when I realised I had to.

I was nine, playing at a friend's house—running through the garden, shrieking with laughter, the way children are supposed to. For a few hours, I forgot who I was.

I was supposed to sleep over. I had packed my pyjamas, my toothbrush. My friend's mother had even set out a spare blanket on the floor.

But then He arrived.

My father.

He smiled politely, shook hands, thanked them for having me. And then, in that smooth, practised voice, He said, "She's been naughty. I'm taking her home."

I hadn't done anything wrong. But I knew better than to argue.

The car ride was silent. My stomach twisted with the familiar dread—the sinking weight of knowing what was coming.

That night, I lay frozen in bed, staring at the door. My heart pounded in my chest as I saw the shadow move from the gap between the door and the floor. I squeezed my eyes shut, willing myself to disappear.

Instead of being at the sleepover with my friends, I was back in my usual nightmare.

When I asked why my brothers didn't have to do the things I did, my father replied, "Because they're boys."

That was all the explanation I got.

In my child's mind, I interpreted it to mean something about me was different. That I wasn't worth the same kind of protection. That I didn't matter the way they did.

I had to find a way to survive.

When He entered the room, I disappeared into The Enchanted Wood. I climbed onto the branches of the Faraway Tree, stepping through magical doorways that led to places where childhood was happy and safe.

In those lands, I wasn't afraid. I was looked after, adored, tucked in at night by parents who whispered, "We love you, sweetheart."

There, when I made a mistake, I wasn't scolded. There, my feelings mattered. There, if I cried, my mother would hold me. She would make me hot chocolate with marshmallows.

There, I was safe.

There, I was loved.

Sometimes I would imagine the smell of cookies baking through the trees, or the warmth of a fire crackling beside me. I'd wrap myself in an invisible blanket of make-believe and float above my body, where He couldn't reach me.

I wanted to stay in that world forever. But of course, I always had to come back.

I didn't know how long He was in the room. Time became strange—stretched and blurry, like it folded in on itself. Minutes felt like hours. I would stare at the polystyrene ceiling tiles to anchor myself, whispering stories in my head to drown out the real one playing out beside me.

Sometimes I'd drift back into the Faraway Tree, holding tightly to the pictures in my mind. I imagined myself climbing higher, past the clouds, until I reached Moon-Face's round room at the top. He was always there—smiling, kind, silly enough to make me laugh.

The door would click shut behind Him. I would lie there, staring at the ceiling, the smell of Him and stale tobacco still clinging to my skin.

And eventually, I'd fall asleep sucking my thumb through tears.

4

THE WEDDING AND THE SHAME THAT FOLLOWED

I was fourteen the night I ruined the wedding. At least, that's what they told me.

The first part of the evening was fun. My cousins and I played a game—swiping beers, spirits and wine while the adults weren't looking. Every time we managed to grab a drink, we burst into laughter, giddy with our own cleverness.

I tried one, then another. It made me feel warm, light, like I had floated out of my body.

The next thing I could remember, I was outside. My head in someone's lap. The cold air against my face. Hands gripping my arms, holding me up. Voices arguing in Croatian.

"She's going to have to go to hospital," I heard one voice say to another.

"No, no—just get her in the car."

Then... darkness.

When I woke up the next morning at my aunt's house,

my mouth was dry, my stomach twisting. But it wasn't just the hangover.

It was the weight of what was coming.

I had embarrassed the family. I had ruined the wedding.

They didn't ask if I was okay. They didn't ask *why* I had gotten so drunk.

They just told me what a disgrace I was.

"You made a fool of yourself."

"The whole family was watching."

"You ruined everything."

The shame settled deep inside me.

It was nothing new.

Later that week, my father told me I had to go to confession. *Why was my dad so upset? Had I said something in my drunken state that would expose Him?*

I sat in the dim light of the confessional, my hands clenched in my lap. The wooden partition separated me from the priest, but I could still feel his presence, waiting.

"Bless me, Father, for I have sinned."

The words came out flat, automatic.

What was I even confessing? That I drank? That I embarrassed them? That I had let the mask slip, just for one night?

"I was mean to my brother," I lied.

It wasn't like my parents were in the confessional with me. I would just pretend I had asked for forgiveness for the wedding incident. *I wondered if my dad goes to confession for the things He was doing to me?*

I hope God understands why I made it up, that I was mean to my brother. Will God be angry that I am lying in confession?

After the wedding, I learnt what not to do.

Don't stand out.

Don't draw attention to myself.

Don't let them see the cracks.

I wasn't going to be the family embarrassment again.

The shame settled deep in my being. And once it was there, it never really left.

By the time I was fifteen, I stopped pretending I didn't know it was wrong.

But if I'm honest, part of me had known for a long time.

There were moments—even years earlier—when my body knew, even if my mind wasn't ready to admit it.

I lived in that in-between space: not quite knowing, not quite unknowing. A place where I told myself it was normal, or not that bad, or maybe just something that happened to girls like me.

I knew what He was doing was wrong.

I knew it wasn't love.

But I also knew that knowing changed nothing.

So I found ways to protect myself.

5

SURVIVAL TACTICS AND TEENAGE YEARS

I was now in puberty. My body was changing, but I didn't feel like I was becoming a woman—I felt like more of a target.

So I fought back the only way I could.

I started wearing pads even when I wasn't bleeding—a silent shield, a desperate excuse.

"I can't, I'm on my period."

Sometimes it worked. Sometimes He left me alone.

Other times, I had to find new excuses.

"I have a stomachache."

"I have a headache."

"I have homework to do."

I got better at avoiding Him —timing my showers, making sure we were never alone.

But no excuse could last forever.

By the time I was sixteen, the walls of my home felt smaller, closing in on me like a cage.

My friends were allowed out—late-night parties, weekend trips to town, laughter spilling through the streets like freedom itself. But for me, the answer was always no.

"Too dangerous."

"Too late."

"You don't need to go out. We can just watch Blind Date."

Other girls had parents who reminded them to be careful, who set curfews but still let them explore the world. My parents didn't believe in curfews because they didn't believe in freedom.

I watched as my friends started planning their futures, choosing universities far from home, imagining new cities, new possibilities.

The thought of leaving became my private obsession. I could get out. I could disappear into a life where I made my own choices.

The more I thought about it, the more desperate I became.

If I could just make it to university, I could be free.

A Body That Wasn't Mine

At home, I perfected the art of avoidance. I learnt to make myself invisible; I'd mastered the art of appearing too busy, too sick, too unavailable.

Being touched was always worse than touching Him. When I was in control—if you could call it that—I could shut my mind off, disappear inside myself, get it over with. But when his hands were on me, I felt powerless. My skin would crawl. I hated it.

And yet, we still went to Mass every Sunday. We were devoted churchgoers—you had to be practically dying to miss Mass.

I remember Holy Week being an endurance test: Ash Wednesday, Maundy Thursday, Good Friday, the Easter vigil on Saturday and finally, Easter Sunday.

The chocolate eggs felt like hard-earned rewards after the week's spiritual marathon.

The Criticism That Shaped Me

If I wasn't being controlled, I was being corrected.

Guska. Stupid.

My mother's voice wasn't just a sound; it was an erosion.

She never told me I was smart. Never said she was proud of me. Never encouraged me.

My efforts were met with disapproval. My mistakes were met with insults.

"You're so clumsy."

"Why can't you do anything right?"

"You are so ugly."

Each word chipped away at something inside me, something fragile but essential.

I longed for tenderness. For kindness. For a mother who would tell me she loved me, who would see me.

But love, in our house, was something unspoken.

So, I did the only thing I could. I planned my escape. I would be out in the world on my own, making my own rules and living in freedom. I wasn't sure what salvation really meant anymore, but I knew it wasn't this.

Then there was the boy I had a crush on. We went for a cycle together to the park. We stopped under a tree that was a bit out of sight of the other park users.

I let him kiss me. His lips were warm, his hands firm, moving down my body. It was my first consensual encounter. Then his fingers started moving lower. Toward the place I never wanted to be touched.

And I froze.

My heart pounded, that familiar feeling of crawling skin. I just laid there. Still. Silent. It was like part of me slipped away. My body stayed under that tree, but my spirit—the real me—was somewhere far off, floating out of reach.

It was something I had learnt without even realising — how to leave myself when it got too scary to stay.

Then, suddenly, I came rushing back. I pulled away.

"I—I have to go," I mumbled as I stood up.

I didn't wait for him to respond. I just turned around and cycled off with tears in my eyes.

I kept replaying the moment in my mind, trying to understand why I reacted that way.

Other girls would have liked it. *Other girls* wouldn't have panicked.

But I wasn't like the *other girls*.

I had already taught myself how to go numb. How to cut off from the parts of me that were too hurt and scared for me to deal with at that time. And this was just one more thing I buried deep. And who could I tell, anyhow? So, I told no one about the incident with the boy under the tree.

After that day, I knew something was wrong with me.

Other girls wanted to be touched. *Other girls* giggled about boys. *Other girls* were *normal.*

But me? I felt disgusted. Dirty. Wrong.

I told myself it was because I was shy. Because I was ugly. Because of the glasses.

I hated wearing glasses.

I had begged my parents to let me try contact lenses. But of course, I was stupid for even asking.

"You look fine in glasses," my mother said. "We can't afford to waste money on something so unnecessary."

Ugly. Clumsy. Stupid.

Those words had settled inside me, shaping and defining the way I saw myself, the way I carried myself. I started to believe that no one would ever want me anyway. So maybe it didn't matter that I couldn't stand to be touched. I pushed it all away. The kiss. The shame. The weird feeling in my stomach that I just couldn't name. The university acceptance letters were coming. And soon, I would be leaving.

Choosing My Way Out

By the time I began sixth form, I had a singular focus: to get out.

I had one requirement: Every university I applied to had to be far enough away that I could not commute from home.

At school, I had never been the most focused student. My mind was always scattered, always somewhere else. My school report would say *"Could Try Harder."*

But something shifted when I realised that getting good grades meant getting away.

So I forced myself to concentrate. I tried to focus on lessons. I started revising. I worked harder. My freedom would be well worth the effort.

While my friends were dating, laughing and flirting without a second thought, I always felt like I was watching from the outside. I just wanted to be normal; to be like them.

6

UNIVERSITY AND THE ESCAPE INTO ALCOHOL

My first love was alcohol. At university, I discovered my superpower—or so I thought. I had made it one hundred miles north of London, to Leicester. Far enough, I believed, to leave my old life behind and finally start over.

After a couple of pints, I had a confidence I'd never felt in my life. I could talk to anyone. The shy girl disappeared. I thought I'd found the key to overcoming my awkwardness, my self-consciousness, my invisibility.

The British '90s ladette culture didn't help. The pubs were smoky, loud and alive with the laughter of students who seemed fearless. Oasis, Pulp and Suede blared from jukeboxes. Drinking wasn't just a social norm—it was expected. The culture practically demanded boozing as a badge of honour—especially for women trying to prove they could keep up with the lads. And I wore that badge with pride.

The Party Girl Who Didn't Remember

If you had asked me as a young adult about my childhood, I would have shrugged.

"Yeah, my parents were strict. Catholic. You know how it is."

And that would have been the end of it.

I didn't consciously decide to forget. It was more like my mind tucked it all away, locking it in some room I didn't even know existed. The memories stayed hidden, outside of my reach, like they belonged to someone else.

Looking back, I wonder—was it unconscious? Or was it pure survival?

Maybe a bit of both. But my body never forgot.

I still hated being touched. I still flinched at certain voices, certain smells. But I had no idea why.

So I did what worked best.

I drank.

Liquid Courage

My taste buds had been trained to like lager. At £1 a pint, I couldn't go wrong.

Getting drunk was cheap. It was fun. And for the first time in my life, I felt free. It was one big party. The clubs in town had student nights during the week and clubbing trumped studying every time.

Having been hungover at most of my lectures over four years, my university studies had been pushed to the bottom of the pile.

But I had one hell of a time at University. So many of my

conversations began with: *"You won't believe what I did last night,"* and *"I was so drunk..."*

So much of my identity had become interwoven with alcohol, it wasn't clear who I *really* was underneath it all. I had adopted the persona of the party girl: the life and soul of the night, the last to leave the scene. But in reality, I was just masking my pain. Had I taken a closer look, I would have seen that my soul was far from happy.

The Art of Forgetting, Perfected

Looking back, I wonder:

Was I always this wild? Or was I just running?

I never had flashbacks. Never had nightmares. Never thought about my past.

It was as if it never happened.

I didn't know that trauma doesn't stay buried forever.

I had unknowingly hit pause.

But my repression could only serve as a temporary plaster; ten years after I began university, I would start remembering.

And once I did, there was no stopping this tsunami.

For now, though?

Another pint, please.

7

BULLYING AT WORK AND THE BREAKDOWN

By the time I had reached my mid-twenties, I had my first permanent job and thought I was finally stepping into adulthood. What I didn't realise was that I was stepping into another cage—just a different kind.

My early working life provided me with a false sense of security. As a temp, I floated between jobs, never staying long enough for anyone to affect me deeply. No office politics. No attachments. Just a weekly pay cheque and an exit whenever I needed one.

But my first permanent position changed everything.

I didn't realise I was essentially signing my life away—stepping into what would become years of subtle torture.

Bullying at work doesn't happen overnight. It begins like water dripping —subtle at first, then relentless. Unstoppable. Before I knew it, I was drowning.

It started subtly. A workload so heavy it was impossible to complete. Requests that seemed designed to set me up for failure. My supervisor, always watching, waiting for a mistake. Then, when I somehow managed to keep up, she changed tactics. Responsibilities were slowly stripped away until I was left with mindless, menial tasks.

Distributing mail.

Photocopying.

Filing papers like I was invisible.

I convinced myself this was normal. That maybe I wasn't cut out for the job. That if I just worked harder, I would prove myself. But bullies don't pick on the strongest—they choose the ones they know won't fight back.

And I had spent my whole life not fighting back.

The Slow Destruction of Self-Worth

The bullying began as a quiet drip. Each incident seemed minor in isolation, but together they formed a waterfall of devastation. My supervisor—lazy but clever—knew exactly how to target someone with low self-worth. She wouldn't dare pick on the confident ones; bullies are cowards who seek out the vulnerable.

One morning, I found my Mr Men toys shoved into my desk drawer.

"This isn't a kindergarten," my supervisor sneered.

I hadn't broken any office rules—Mr Happy who sat by my computer made me smile. Now he and the others were banished to the bottom drawer.

I should have stood up for myself. I should have walked away. But instead, I swallowed the humiliation, forced a tight-lipped smile and carried on.

That's what I had always done—kept quiet, made myself smaller, remained invisible.

Crying in the Office Toilets

Soon, I was crying in the bathroom at work, my stomach in knots before each workday. But not even this would trigger any awareness inside myself that something was wrong. I just kept going, numbing myself with alcohol in the evenings, stumbling through hungover days and repeat.

The question I'd later ask myself repeatedly was:

"Why didn't I just leave this job?"

But that's the insidious nature of low self-esteem—it convinces you that you don't deserve better. That this is all you're worth.

I couldn't even make basic decisions without seeking the approval of others, having lost all trust in my own judgement. I clung to basic admin work that was being stripped away, convincing myself that this was all I could handle.

Depression crept in silently. Weekends became a refuge best spent from under the covers, avoiding life. Even dancing, once a source of joy, left me feeling empty. The British stiff upper lip kept me going, but at what cost?

Glimmers of Joy, Stamped Out

There were brief moments of joy—like the day Goran Ivanišević won Wimbledon. My brothers and I slept on the pavement to get tickets, celebrated with Australian fans and were interviewed on TV. For a moment, I felt free. For a moment, I felt alive. But even this victory turned sour.

Sleeping on the pavement had left me with a lingering back injury, which meant I had to take a few days off from work. When I returned, my supervisor used my absence as ammunition against me—extending my probation and putting me on performance review. No matter what I did, I would never be good enough.

Same Patterns, Different Places

My relationships outside of work reflected the same pattern of low self-worth.

When a colleague asked to borrow money I really couldn't spare, I took out a credit card loan to help her. When a date stood me up twice with increasingly unlikely excuses about his father's health, I blamed myself.

I had no sense of self. No boundaries. My entire identity was blurred with others' expectations and demands. I thought I was just bad at my job. That if I could be perfect, they would finally approve of me. But deep down, I wasn't trying to win their approval. I was replaying something much older. The feeling of never being good enough wasn't born in that office. It had long been with me, dating back to childhood.

The Unfinished Lesson

When you grow up believing your needs don't matter—that your voice is a disruption—you carry that with you into adulthood.

You tolerate what you shouldn't.

You mistake mistreatment for normality.

I wasn't just surviving a toxic workplace—I was living out the lessons my childhood had taught me.

A New Escape

As an adult, drinking had always been my escape. My first love. My social armour. It gave me the confidence I never had as a child and the reckless abandon I thought I needed to survive adulthood.

But even alcohol had its limits. The hangovers were getting worse. By the time I was in my late twenties, the energy it took to keep up the party girl persona was draining me. The laughter felt forced, the nights out blurred together and somewhere beneath the surface, I could sense that something inside me was unravelling.

I wasn't ready to face it. Not yet.

And then I found cannabis.

It felt different—light, detached, as if I was floating just above myself, untouchable. Where alcohol had been wild and messy, cannabis was softer, quieter. Like wrapping myself in a warm blanket and muting the world.

It all started innocently enough. I had moved into a flatshare where everyone smoked and at first it was just a social thing—a puff here, a shared joint after dinner. A way to unwind after work.

But soon, it wasn't just after work. It was before work. It was on my lunch break. It was creeping into every corner of my life, numbing the parts of me I wasn't ready to look at.

I told myself it was harmless. That everyone did it. That I was just taking the edge off. And at first, it worked. Work was unbearable, my self-esteem was in tatters and the bullying hadn't stopped. Smoking took that feeling away—at least for a little while.

But the more I relied on it, the more I had to hide it.

I started chewing gum before walking into the office, paranoid that the smell would give me away. I timed my smoke breaks carefully, making sure my eyes wouldn't be too red for meetings. I convinced myself that I had it under control.

But deep down, I knew. I knew that once again, I was trying to outrun something I couldn't even name yet.

And just like drinking, it would only work until it didn't.

8

THE MEMORIES RETURN

For years, I kept going. Kept my head down. Kept trying.

Work was unbearable, yet I told myself to push through. Everyone had bad days, didn't they? I convinced myself I was just being dramatic. That I needed to toughen up. That if I could just be better—work harder, complain less, get everything right—things would improve.

But things never improved. They got worse.

The bullying at work had become relentless. I had always had to endure and survive. I thought I could swallow this too. But then, the past started creeping back in.

It happened in small flashes at first—small, unwelcome images slipping through the cracks of my carefully constructed denial. A touch. A smell. The weight of a shadow at my bedroom door. I would shake my head, physically trying to dislodge the memories. But they kept on coming.

At night, I could barely sleep. When I did, I dreamt of

hands where they shouldn't be. Of being frozen in place, unable to scream.

I'd be at my desk during the day, pretending to work, when suddenly I wasn't in the office anymore—I was seven years old, trapped in a bedtime story that had turned into a real-life horror show.

I had spent ten years unknowingly burying it all. And there, without warning, my mind had decided it was time to remember.

It was too much.

One day, in a meeting, my boss wouldn't stop staring at me. I asked if I could present my ideas tomorrow—I wasn't feeling well. I didn't know it then, but that would be the last time I ever saw her.

Tears blurred my vision. My hands trembled. I barely made it onto the tube. The next day, I called in sick.

I was so disconnected from myself that I only went to the doctor because I'd phoned in sick and needed a sick note.

At the doctor's surgery, I expected to be told I was fine. That I just needed rest. A vitamin deficiency, maybe iron tablets. Something small. Something fixable.

But instead, the doctor looked at me with great concern. *"I'm worried you're on the verge of a breakdown."*

I wasn't coping. I had been pretending for so long, I had started believing my own lies.

He signed me off work for two months. Two months turned into six. Six turned into a year. A year turned into the government supporting me with Incapacity Benefit—a lifeline for those too unwell to work.

During this time, I had no choice but to stop denying my

past. Stop the endless tirade of lies and distractions I'd been imposing upon myself.

And once I did, everything I had been running from finally caught up with me.

Three Weeks of Crying

With nowhere else to turn, I went to stay with my friend Jessica at Greenbanks Cottage in the quiet village of Mitcheldean. I told her I needed rest. That I was burnt out from the bullying. I didn't have the courage to tell her the truth—that memories of childhood abuse had begun to surface and I was breaking under the weight of them.

The moment I arrived, I cried. Not just tears, but inconsolable, guttural sobs that came flooding out from where they had been buried deep for so long. I cried so hard and so often that entire days would pass in a blur. Between crying cycles, I slept. It was as if my body had finally collapsed under the weight of my years as a self-inflicted imposter.

Jessica held me in her arms, day after day, just as I wished my mother would, as I sobbed without words. I couldn't speak about what was happening—not yet. The pain was still too raw, too fragmented to form sentences. All I could do was weep. The only sounds in the house were my cries and the soft rustling of Dezmond, her house rabbit, hopping softly past like a quiet companion.

My friend's brother, Eon, came to stay for a few nights. He sat with me and held me as I cried through the night. There were no questions, no demands for explanation—just quiet presence, something I hadn't even known I needed. It was the first time I had been allowed to fall apart safely.

Those three weeks were a blur of tears and exhaustion—the quiet unravelling of a previously inexpressible truth, the pain flooding through the cracks.

Losing Trust in the World

At first, I tried to fight it. I had filed a grievance against my boss, believing that justice would win. That fairness existed. That someone would acknowledge what had happened to me. But the investigation dragged on for months. When the final decision came back, my heart sank: *No evidence of bullying.*

I appealed. Months later, the second decision arrived: *No evidence of bullying.* I was devastated.

The organisation had taken no responsibility. I was left with nothing—no job, no justice, no sense of closure.

Any trust I had left in humanity, in fairness, in the idea that good would triumph over evil, had been shattered. I had spent my life believing if I just followed the rules, if I could just be a good girl, things would work out for me.

But that was a lie. No one was coming to save me.

I stopped trusting people. I barely spoke to anyone. During the day, I wandered around parks, booze in one hand, a joint in the other. I didn't know what I was doing. I didn't know who I was.

Then one day, while I was alone in the park, the loneliness that came over me had become unbearable. My hands trembled as I reached for another can of cheap lager—my afternoon drinking, a worrying new addition to my repertoire of missteps.

I decided to ring the Samaritans. That's what people did when they had no one to talk to, wasn't it? When they were at rock bottom?

I picked up my mobile and dialled the number.

A voice, gentle and patient, answered. Suddenly, I had a flashback to being in the phone box as a child, unable to speak. Decades later, I had finally found my voice.

"Do you listen to messed-up things?" I asked. My voice was barely above a whisper.

"Go on," she said softly.

"I was sexually abused as a child."

The words felt foreign in my mouth, like they belonged to someone else. I expected the world to shift, for the sky to darken, for something—anything—to change.

The park was quiet except for a few birds singing. The Samaritan lady asked if I had told anyone else. When I said no, she urged me to confide in someone I trusted. *"Tell your brother,"* she suggested.

My immediate response was automatic, revealing the weight I had been carrying my entire life:

"I can't destroy my family."

I wasn't protecting myself—I was protecting them. This was my burden to carry.

Breaking the Silence

It would take six more months before I told another soul.

On holiday with my brother, drowning in more alcohol than usual, the Samaritan lady's words echoed in my mind.

"Tell someone you trust."

Through tears, I finally spoke His name. I said it out loud. The name of the man who had stolen my childhood.

My brother's face turned pale as he listened. Hearing that his own father had abused his sister, he had no manual for handling such a revelation. But the words had been spoken. There was no taking them back.

Then something shifted in me. It wasn't a miracle. It didn't erase the years of pain. But for the first time, I wasn't carrying this burden alone.

I felt *relief*.

The shame, the secrecy, the years of silence—I had been bearing the weight on my shoulders alone for so long. But just by saying it, some of that load had lifted off of me.

Telling the Samaritan lady had been like whispering into a void—safe, but distant.

But telling my brother? That was real. That was raw truth stepping out into the light. For the first time, I truly felt like maybe, just maybe, I wouldn't have to carry this alone forever.

Now That I Knew, What Was I Supposed to Do?

Knowing the truth should have changed everything. But it didn't. Not really.

Yes, I now knew my father was my abuser. Yes, I had said the words out loud. But knowing wasn't the same as healing.

And I did not want to deal with this. I wanted it to go away. So, I kept running. Running from the memories, from the shame, from the crushing weight of what I had buried for so long.

And then, I discovered self-help books.

9
HEALING STEPS

The first time I saw *Invisible Girls* in the bookshop, my stomach fluttered. I wanted to reach for it. I wanted to read the words of someone who might understand what had happened to me.

But what if someone saw? What if my flatmates found it? What if the cashier gave me a strange look? I couldn't risk it. I couldn't risk being seen.

So instead of buying it, I started reading it in secret—in stolen increments, standing in the self-help section, heart pounding, eyes darting around to make sure no one was watching.

Each time, I flipped through a few pages, absorbing just enough before sliding it back onto the shelf, pretending to browse.

It was as if even owning the book would expose me. As if carrying it home would make it real in a way I wasn't ready for.

But I kept going back.

Something in me needed those words—even if I could only take them in small doses.

I was comforted by the realisation that it wasn't just me. I wasn't the only one who had been through such an experience. There were others—women who had lived through it, who had found the words I still couldn't say, who had survived.

The book that I did end up buying was Louise Hay's *You Can Heal Your Life*. This one didn't scream "trauma victim" to me. It was about positive thinking, affirmations and changing your life. No one would guess my secret if they saw that one on my shelf. It was my first step into self-help, though I didn't know it then. A tiny seed of hope planted in a mind still tangled in shame.

Maybe I Didn't Have to Heal, Maybe I Could Make Him Disappear

As I explored self-help books, I stumbled upon something even more intriguing: manifestation.

I had never heard of it before, but the idea fascinated me. The books said I could manifest anything I wanted—money, love, success.

But I didn't care about money.

I wanted Him gone.

What if I could manifest his death? Would the universe comply with my instruction? If I visualised hard enough, if I truly believed, would He just... die?

That would fix everything, wouldn't it? Surely, I would be free.

The Ritual That Didn't Work

They tell you to be specific when making a request to the universe. So I was.

I sketched a tombstone. His name. His date of birth. His date of death.

I gave the universe one month to make it happen. That would give the higher forces enough time to act and set up my request.

I waited.

And then, the date arrived.

And of course He did not die.

Nothing changed.

He was still alive.

And I was still trapped in the nightmare I had spent my whole life trying to escape.

What Now?

If even the universe couldn't save me, how the hell was I supposed to save myself? I still wasn't ready to face it—not really. I wasn't ready to heal. So I did the only thing I knew how to do. I kept on running. In my effort to avoid the past, I ended up manifesting my own haunting, where I remained shackled to my trauma, like one's own executioner.

Chasing Love in All the Wrong Places

Amidst all the chaos, I fell for someone who had no interest in a relationship with me.

He didn't want commitment and I told myself that was fine.

I agreed to a no-strings arrangement, convincing myself I was the kind of girl who didn't need labels. That I wasn't looking for love anyway.

But I was lying to myself.

Because what I really wanted wasn't sex—it was the moments after. The cuddles. The warmth. The feeling of being held, even if it meant nothing to him. That's what the broken girl inside of me wanted. So I let him use me, thinking that maybe if I gave him my body, he might eventually want the rest of me too.

Of course, that was never going to happen. But I clung to the scraps of his attention, convinced that if I waited long enough, if I played it cool, if I tried hard enough, it would turn into something real.

And then one night, as I lay awake in his bed, listening to him snore beside me, something inside me stirred.

It wasn't dramatic or loud—just a whisper.

This isn't love.
You deserve more.

It was my voice—quiet, but certain.

10

THE CRASH THAT SHOOK ME AWAKE

Following months of isolation, filled with endless days spent wandering through parks, numbing myself with alcohol and weed, I stumbled across an opportunity to volunteer at a workplace bullying charity. I was desperate to find meaning in what had happened to me—to transform my pain into something useful. Workplace bullying had contributed to my shattered trust and helping others navigate that same darkness felt like a lifeline, a tiny thread connecting me back to the world.

I became obsessed. I immersed myself in research, determined to understand every aspect of workplace bullying. It consumed my thoughts, my days, my entire existence. If I could help others, maybe it would help me, too.

Then, one evening after volunteering, as I was driving back from Slough along the M4, listening to Snow Patrol's "Run" playing on the radio, *it* happened. One moment I was driving, the next, the world exploded around me.

A skidding of tyres. A sudden flash of brake lights. My foot slammed instinctively on the brake pedal, but it had been too late. There were crushing sounds of metal colliding and screeching tyres. I felt a violent and forceful jolt as my car slammed into the vehicle ahead. Glass shattered around me as I hit my head on the steering wheel. My car was old, without an airbag.

Time slowed down, stretched out in painful clarity. For a moment, I hung suspended, my body pinned, with the sound of Snow Patrol still whispering faintly beneath the chaos.

Then... darkness.

When I opened my eyes again, fluorescent lights glared harshly above me. My body ached, every muscle protesting as I tried to move. A doctor stood by my bedside, clipboard in hand, his face gentle but serious.

"You're incredibly lucky," he said softly. "Accidents like this usually have far worse outcomes."

Lucky.

The word echoed strangely. *Lucky* to be lying bruised and shaken in a hospital bed? *Lucky* to have narrowly escaped death?

But he was right.

As I laid there in the sterile silence of the hospital room, reality washed over me—undeniable and sobering.

I had been spiralling for months. Trying to make sense of what had happened at work had become my full-time obsession—an attempt to find meaning, to feel in control, to stop the noise in my head.

But instead of healing me, it had consumed me.

The darkness I'd been drowning in had finally taken form—violent, sudden, impossible to ignore.

I was later told the emergency responders had to cut me out of my Fiat Cinquecento while I laid there, unconscious.

The accident was my wake-up call. I couldn't let the bullying define me anymore; it had almost killed me.

I wasn't just driving home that night—I was driving myself into the ground.

I'd been obsessively trying to understand workplace bullying, unable to let go, pouring everything I had into an unpaid volunteer role. I thought I was helping others, but really, I was stuck. I wasn't healing. I wasn't moving on. I was just reliving the pain, over and over again, until it finally caught up with me.

I had to get on with my life. I had to move forward.

The crash had jolted me out of my paralysis, forcing me to see that I had a choice: I could keep living in the shadows of what happened, or I could take control of my own story.

Yet, knowing I needed to move forward didn't mean I knew how. The accident had made clear that I couldn't return to the old ways, the old patterns.

But what alternative did I have? My mind scrambled for answers, but every pathway I could see led back to the same bleak destination: the suffocating confinement of office work.

Lost and Searching

At this point in my life, I was completely lost. The idea of ever returning to office work filled me with horror. My entire professional life had been spent trapped behind desks, moving paperwork, answering phones, being quietly undermined by my boss. But what else could I do? My CV was nothing but office jobs; a trail of experiences I never wanted to revisit.

But maybe I didn't have to. Could I retrain? Could I choose a different path?

As I wrestled with this uncertainty, a long-forgotten memory emerged with vivid clarity: I was fourteen again, sitting at a worn wooden desk, my fountain pen hovering over a list of GCSE subjects. My eyes scanned the list, eager and hopeful. Physical Education was the first thing that jumped out. Sports had always been a source of joy for me. But my father said it was a useless subject and forced me to pick something else.

I wondered, *could I reclaim that lost dream*?

For the first time in years, I felt a spark of optimism. I began researching and exploring my options. The possibility of retraining—of pursuing something meaningful to me—filled me with hope. Perhaps it wasn't too late.

Hope, Almost Lost

For the first time, I felt excited—energised, even. Perhaps I could reclaim something from my past. Personal training—it felt perfect. A chance to reconnect with the child who had once loved running and jumping, who found freedom in movement.

Then I saw the price: £4,000.

My heart sank. How had I even allowed myself to dream? I was on Incapacity Benefit, barely covering my rent, alcohol and smokes. Four thousand pounds might as well have been four million. The audacity of my momentary dream had become instantly rattled by the cold, hard reality.

A Glimmer of Possibility

The next morning, something nudged me back to the library. I stumbled upon something called a Career Development Loan. You could apply to banks for a career development loan, specifically for retraining. It seemed too simple to be real, but I took a leap of faith. My hands trembled as I clicked on the application link. I filled out the form and submitted it. Faced with a three to six weeks waiting period before hearing of the outcome, it would be the longest wait of my life.

Then, four weeks later, an envelope arrived: *Congratulations! Your Career Development Loan application has been approved.*

For the first time in years, genuine, unadulterated joy surged through me. Maybe, just maybe, my life wasn't over. Maybe, there was more in store for me in this life.

Finding Yoga

Around the same time, I had read that yoga could be utilised as a healing practice, so I thought, *let's give it a go.* My first class was interesting. The teacher started the class with a chant: "Om shanti, Om Shanti, peace, peace, peace."

What kind of weirdness was this? I had never heard of a mantra before and the teacher explained it as a way of affirming and wishing for peace internally and externally.

Great—give me some of *that*. My internal world was a battlefield, thoughts crashing into one another like waves in a storm. If anyone could've seen inside my head, they would've fled.

A Year of Persistence

The personal training course was supposed to take three months. For me, it took a year.

I had been prescribed antidepressants after being signed off work—and the doctor gently suggested I begin counselling as well.

"Medication can help," he said, "but it won't do the work for you. You need to get to the root of it."

I didn't fully understand what he meant at the time, but something in me knew he was right. So I agreed.

Therapy had begun, slowly unpicking the tangled knots of trauma inside me. I had a new diagnosis: complex PTSD. A part of me felt relieved—it had a name. But another part resisted, afraid of what facing it would mean.

Everyday tasks felt overwhelming. Concentrating for long periods was nearly impossible. Anxiety made my mind race and freeze at the same time. Some days, just getting out of bed felt like a battle I barely won. It had been no wonder the course dragged on far beyond the expected timeline.

I was determined to move my life forward. I stumbled through exams, failing more than I passed. After every failure, the voice in my head whispered, "See, you're worthless. You're stupid. *Guska*." But something deeper—something stronger—had awakened within me: a stubborn refusal to give up.

Taking antidepressants helped, softening the edge of my overwhelming sadness. Yoga classes became a lifeline; moments where I glimpsed a peaceful version of myself. But old habits clung to me stubbornly. I still smoked weed—one hand reaching for healing, the other still tethered to my old ways.

But I kept going. I wasn't going to fix everything all at once, but I was taking steps in the right direction. After each setback, I studied harder, practised longer, retook exams with gritted teeth and determination. And then one day, finally, I'd reached the finish line.

"Congratulations. You've successfully passed your final exam. You are now a certified Personal Trainer and Sports Massage Therapist."

I stared at the words on my computer screen, reading them over and over again as tears streamed down my face. I did it. A three-month course had taken me a full year, but I had done it.

This victory belonged to a girl who had spent a lifetime believing she couldn't achieve anything—a girl who once hid behind alcohol, weed and self-loathing. Now here I was, holding proof in black and white that my past didn't have to define my future.

The words blurred as tears of relief filled my eyes. For the first time in a long time, I felt proud. I was qualified, I was capable and I was enough.

Afraid to Charge My Worth

I could then call myself a qualified personal trainer. But every time I thought about actually charging clients, I panicked. £50 an hour? Would they think I was ripping them off, asking for a fee that high? Who the hell did I think I was?

I imagined standing in front of a client, clipboard in hand, pretending I knew what I was doing. The thought alone made me want to crawl back under my duvet.

The truth was, I didn't feel ready. Not to sell myself. Not to market my services. Not to stand in front of someone and confidently say, "Yes, I am worth this."

Because deep down, I didn't believe I was. So, I did what I had always done—I found the safest option.

Starting from the Bottom

Instead of launching straight into personal training, I applied for a job as a fitness instructor at a gym. It wasn't glamorous. It paid just above minimum wage. But it was something.

And surprisingly, I loved it.

I wrote client programmes, walked the gym floor and chatted with members about their goals. I got to dip my toes in the world of fitness without the pressure of selling myself. One of the other instructors encouraged me to do a group cycle class qualification. It was only a day course and an assessment. I decided to go for it and soon I was teaching a group cycle class. I loved it: the music, the sweat and the endorphin rush. Things were getting better.

11

THE PRICE OF SILENCE

I had been avoiding Him for months, dodging family gatherings, burying myself in work... convincing myself that distance was enough.

But distance *wasn't* enough.

Avoidance hadn't erased the memories. It hadn't dulled the anger that had been building inside me like a slow-burning fire.

And then, one day, there He was.

I was walking down the street, lost in my thoughts, when I saw Him. My father. The man who had stolen my childhood. Just standing there, as if He were any other person. As if He were normal. As if He hadn't ruined me.

Something inside of me snapped.

Before I knew it, I was in front of Him.

"How could you? I was a child!" I spat, my voice shaking with fury.

He turned, confused at first. And then He saw me.

"Daniela," He said, his tone neutral, as if we were just two acquaintances crossing paths.

That only made it worse.

All those years of silence, all the times I had to wash Him while He lay in the bath and do what no child should ever have to do.

I could tell He knew what I was talking about. "Please forgive me. God forgives and so can you."

This made my blood boil as He mentioned God. "How could you do something so sinful?" I screamed.

My fists connected with his chest, his shoulders, his face. Years of anger, shame and helplessness poured out of me in every strike.

"How could you?" I screamed. "How dare you walk around like you're innocent?"

He stumbled back, shocked. I had never hit Him before. I had never fought back.

And I didn't stop.

My fists pounded against Him, my vision blurred by rage, my breath ragged.

"What kind of man can do this to his own daughter?" I hissed.

He flinched but stayed silent.

"You can't be my real father," I spat. "No real father would do this to his own child."

His jaw tightened.

"I am your father," He said, his voice steady. "Of course I am."

"That makes it even worse," I screamed.

Then suddenly, a voice—sharp, reprimanding.

"You can't hit an old man!"

A woman. A stranger. She had stopped on the street, her face twisted in disapproval.

I turned to her, chest heaving, hands shaking.

She had no idea.

No idea at all.

"You know NOTHING," I roared, my voice raw, wild.

She flinched, taking a step back.

People were watching now. The street had gone silent. My father was hunched over, his hands raised, his face a mask of feigned innocence.

And suddenly, it hit me—this wasn't a victory. Punching Him wouldn't undo the past. It wouldn't take back what He did. It wouldn't heal me.

I stepped away, my whole body trembling. The rage that had consumed me left a hollow ache in its place.

I turned and walked away, leaving Him there.

Why can't He just die?

The Pretending Act

I had confronted Him. I had screamed in his face, my fists colliding with his chest, his shoulders, his lying mouth. I had let myself feel the rage. And yet, here I was. Sitting across from Him at the dinner table. Pretending.

My mother placed a steaming bowl of soup in front of me. "Eat before it gets cold," she said. I loved my mum's food. I always had.

My father led grace before dinner. Oh, the irony.

I picked up my spoon, forcing my hand to stay steady.

Across from me, He ate as if nothing had happened. As if I hadn't attacked Him in the street a few months back.

As if I hadn't screamed, "You can't be my real father!"

The Bargain I Made with Myself

I told myself it didn't matter.

He was an old man. He would die soon. And then it would be over. I didn't have to rip the family apart. I didn't have to break my mother's heart. I just had to wait. Wait for Him to die. And then I would be free. I would just pretend we were a 'normal Catholic family'.

I rehearsed His funeral in my mind.

I pictured the dark suits, the murmured condolences, the tears that everyone would expect from a Catholic daughter. I could feel the weight of the black dress against my legs, smell the incense filling the church.

I saw myself standing by the coffin, face arranged in sorrow, while inside I felt a sharp, bright joy burning like a secret flame. If He died first, my mum would be a widow—and there is no shame in being a widow. His death would set us free without a scandal, without courtrooms, without anyone knowing what really happened.

I hated myself for wanting it.

I had already tried to manifest His death—sent the request to the universe, pleaded for it in silence—but nothing happened.

The fantasy was easier than ripping the family apart while He still breathed, while His chest still rose and fell with the steady rhythm of someone who might just live forever and prolong my living hell.

The Crossroads: Yoga Teacher or Party Girl?

I loved working at the gym. The pounding music, the rhythm of the workouts, the feeling of movement—it was the one place where my past didn't haunt me. When I was training a client or teaching a circuit class, I was present. Fully, truly present. No ghosts, no memories, no past.

I was loving my work. I was good at it. I was even personal training, slowly starting to believe I was worth more than minimum wage. And then there was yoga. Yoga had been so therapeutic. It was where I found a stillness I didn't know existed inside me. Where I first heard the words, "You are not your thoughts." Where, for brief moments, I felt peace—not the kind found at the bottom of a pint glass or in a hazy cloud of smoke—but real, solid, undeniable peace.

So I made the decision to become a yoga teacher.

The Secret Habit I Couldn't Shake

The course ran on weekends.

I loved it—learning about breath, alignment, the philosophy and principles of yoga. The idea of teaching yoga felt right.

And yet...

At lunchtime, while the other students sat together in cafés, sipping herbal tea, I would disappear. I'd walk through the streets of central London, searching for a quiet alleyway, a hidden bench, a place where I could roll a joint and get just high enough to take the edge off.

What the hell was I doing?

I was training to be a yoga teacher, but I was still hiding. Still escaping.

My hands shook as I lit the joint, inhaling deeply, feeling the familiar calm wash over me. But this time, it didn't feel like relief. It felt like betrayal.

What was I doing? Did I want to be a party girl or a yoga teacher? Because I couldn't be both.

The dissonance was disturbing me. I was moving forward, but I was also still running. From what? From Him? From the memories? From *myself*?

At night, lying in bed, I had a quiet but brutal conversation with myself.

I had already made one bargain—to stay silent for the sake of the family.

I would do nothing.

Say nothing.

Take the secret to the grave.

No one else needed to know.

I would protect everyone.

Even Him.

But would I protect *myself*?

If I was serious about moving forward—serious about healing—and if I were to become the person I was striving to be with all my might. Could I keep carrying this secret? Could I keep getting high? How long could I keep pretending?

I knew that one day, I'd have to choose. Maybe a little sooner than I wanted to.

I could have made more friends at the yoga course if I didn't keep sloping off. I am still chewing gum after a smoke. Does chewing gum even work? Or am I just fooling myself? Can they smell the cannabis on me? Can they tell that in the afternoons I was stoned? Why can't I change? Do I just have an addictive personality? So many questions bounced around my mind, none of which I had the answers to.

The silence surrounding my abuse was not just a personal tragedy, but a carefully maintained facade. We were pillars of the Croatian Catholic community in London. Secrets, I would learn, were the currency of my family.

Little did I know, another revelation was about to unfold—one that would further unravel the complex tapestry of my origins.

12

THE LETTER

"Did you get any letters recently?" my mother asked, her face tight with anxiety.

I frowned. "What letter?"

She backpedaled, forcing a casual tone. "Oh, don't worry, it's nothing."

But her eyes betrayed her. Not even she could mask the strained expression written all over her face.

For weeks, I checked the post religiously. But the mysterious letter never appeared.

I might have forgotten about it entirely if my mother's best friend, Vana, hadn't reached out months later.

Vana was like my second mother. The one person in my childhood who made me feel seen. Years later, I would speak at her funeral, proud to honour her memory until we meet again, in whatever plane that lies beyond.

"I have a letter for you," she said. "Can you come and get it?"

"Who's it from?"

"Please just come and read it."

My mind raced with possibilities. Maybe it was a cheque from a long-lost relative. Maybe it was some old debt catching up with me. The past always has a way of finding you—maybe the student loans company had finally tracked me down.

The envelope bore a Croatian stamp.

I tore it open, hands trembling slightly and found not a fortune waiting for me, but something far more valuable and equally devastating.

A letter from my **biological father**.

The world tilted on its axis. Time slammed to a halt. I read the sentence over and over, unable to make sense of the words on the page. My heart pounded in my ears, my hands trembled and a strange numbness crept up my spine. Nothing in my life made sense anymore.

My brothers were only half-brothers. My abuser wasn't my father.

At first, I felt relief. A strange, unexpected lightness. He wasn't my blood. I was never his.

But that relief quickly twisted into something else—grief, confusion, rage. It didn't make what He did any less cruel. If anything, it added another layer of betrayal.

He had lied to me. For years. He had let me believe I was his daughter. Let me carry his name, his legacy, his shadow. Let me call Him "Tata" while He played the role of both guardian and predator.

I had been so puzzled, trying to make sense of the impossible—how a father could do this to his own child. And now, the most surreal twist: He wasn't even my father to begin with.

Maybe that's what made it worse. It was all a performance. An illusion.

If I had known, maybe I would have spoken out sooner. Maybe I wouldn't have been so afraid to break the silence. Maybe I wouldn't have spent years walking a tightrope between loyalty and self-preservation.

The weight of it pressed down on me—the secrets, the deception, the sheer absurdity of it all. Nothing in my life had been what it seemed. It was all an illusion, a script I had been following without knowing the lines had been written in deceit.

And my mother? She had known. She had known all along. Of course she knew—she was the one who had given birth to me. She knew exactly who my father was.

But if I wasn't his daughter, then why had He married my mother? Had He chosen her because she had a young child? The thought was chilling. I felt sick and I wasn't sure how much more I could take. A cold dread seeped into my being. I wanted to dismiss it, to push it away. But once the question was asked, it refused to leave.

Was I part of a sick plan?

And now—who is this joker claiming to be my biological father?

In the letter, my biological father mentioned his two children, just a few years younger than me. Anger rose like bile in my throat. He had been a father to them, but not to me. He had made space for them in his life while I was left in the dark like a secret he was too ashamed to acknowledge.

He had left me to my fate. Abandoned me to suffer. Cast away in a life with a predator pretending to be my real father.

All those years of Catholic teachings about truth-telling. All those confessions I'd made as a child. Meanwhile, the adults in my life—the ones tasked with caring for me and helping me navigate my place in this world—lived and breathed lies.

The Priest's Daughter

I confronted my mother, watching her face go white when I mentioned the letter.

"I know about my new dad," I said, the words bitter in my mouth.

She burst into tears.

"I wanted to tell you when you were a teenager, but I didn't. And as time went on, it became harder and harder."

"Mum, I'm thirty-one years old. How is it possible I'm only just finding out now?"

"I wanted to keep you," she said, her voice breaking. "It was the best time of my life when it was just you and me. Your father was in a very difficult position. We couldn't be together."

"Why? Was it because he didn't want a child?"

"It was complicated."

"Was he with someone else?"

"Kind of."

"You didn't sleep with a married man?"

"Well, not exactly. He was married to his job."

My stomach clenched. "What does that mean?"

She took a deep breath.

"He was a priest."

The words hit like a punch to the gut.

"A Catholic priest?"

She nodded.

Betrayal Upon Betrayal

Both men who had claimed the title of my father were Catholic priests. One had abandoned me. The other had violated me. The hypocrisy was soul-crushing.

These men, who had stood before congregations preaching about morality, sanctity and the protection of the innocent, had instead embodied the most grotesque betrayal of everything they claimed to represent.

The church had been such a big part of my life growing up—those Sunday masses, the hymns, the rituals—and now it felt like a complete facade.

These men, ordained to serve as spiritual guardians, had instead become predators.

One had sexually abused me, turning sacred trust into a weapon. The other had abandoned me, treating me as an inconvenient secret to be hidden away.

Their collars hadn't made them holy; they had made them more dangerous. This revelation wasn't just about two individual men—it was about an entire system that protected perpetrators, that valued institutional reputation over human suffering.

My understanding of faith, of family, of trust—everything

—had been systematically dismantled by the very people who were supposed to embody spiritual integrity. The betrayal cut so deep it felt like my whole childhood had been a lie. How could men sworn to God's service be capable of such profound moral bankruptcy?

13

MEETING IN TISNO

That summer I was in Croatia, the land of my ancestors. My biological father lived only thirty minutes from where I was staying, in a coastal village called Tisno. Vana had given me his address, her quiet encouragement spurring me forward. Still, I wondered how an unannounced visit from a long-lost daughter would land. Had he thought about me during all these years?

Vana was friends with my biological father maybe that's why he sent the letter to her. Perhaps he was worried that if he sent it to my mum, she'd just throw it away.

As the bus wound its way by the Croatian coastline, I tried not to let my thoughts get ahead of me.

What if he likes me? What if I wasn't just a long-forgotten secret, but someone he actually wants to know?

I wasn't naïve. I knew I shouldn't expect too much. But still, that tiny ember of hope flickered inside me. Maybe this was my chance to finally have a father. Maybe, after everything, I could have something real.

The coach driver dropped me on the main road, suggesting I hitchhike the rest of the way. An elderly man offered me a ride and when I asked for directions, he knew exactly who my father was. I told him I was visiting from England, claiming my mother was a friend of his. In villages like this, news travels faster than wildfire.

Tisno sprawled before me, beautiful and daunting. I climbed the hill in the scorching summer heat, sweat beading on my forehead as the temperature pushed past 35 degrees Celsius. When I found the house, my courage nearly failed me.

What if his wife answered? What if she didn't know about me?

I took a deep breath and knocked on the door. Within seconds, an older man appeared, moving stiffly but without aid. He studied me with curious eyes as I introduced myself.

"Do you know who I am?" I asked finally.

"Yes, I know who you are. You must have got my letter."

I nodded and he glanced behind him before suggesting we go somewhere for a drink. In his car, he touched my shoulder gently.

"I've seen you a few times in your life," he confessed. "You would go to the Croatian church in London with your parents. I wanted so badly to say hello, but your mother would have been furious. Once you smiled at me and I felt my heart melt."

We sat in a café. I wondered if I should tell him the truth

about my childhood. But the words wouldn't come. If my years had taught me anything, it's that other people's comfort mattered more than my truth. So instead, we chatted about safer topics—my life, my half-siblings whom I've never met. He hoped we might meet someday.

When he drove me back to my village, he hugged me tightly and said, "Keep in touch."

I couldn't tell him about the abuse. I questioned why I still felt the need to protect him. But then again, I'd learnt early on that silence was safety and other people's needs outweighed my own.

After our first meeting in Croatia, we saw each other a few more times in London. On one occasion, I invited my dad over for dinner and my then boyfriend, a chef, had planned to cook for us. But that day, work kept him late, so I made dinner instead. *Full disclosure*: my cooking wasn't great back then.

I could feel my dad's disappointment the moment he sat down. It lingered in the air, unspoken but heavy. And then, the following summer in Croatia, he finally put it into words —the ones that ended our already fragile relationship:

"If I had known your boyfriend wasn't going to make dinner that evening, I wouldn't have come."

His words hit me harder than I expected, like a door shutting in my face. I was devastated. It wasn't just about the dinner—it was about me. About how little I mattered.

And then it came: that whisper.

This isn't love. You deserve more.

It was the same whisper I'd heard before; the one that

helped me walk away from the man who wasn't even my boyfriend.

As we parted that day, I knew it would be the last time for a long time—fifteen years, in fact. I was done taking scraps of attention; tired of feeling like a puppy begging for love.

Something inside me was shifting. For the first time, I was beginning to understand: *I deserved better.*

14

BUILDING A NEW LIFE

The day I met my future husband, I was due to meet a friend at a pub to watch the AFC Wimbledon play-off final against Luton Town. If Wimbledon won, they'd return to the Football League—it was a big deal. So I headed to the pub.

I'd just come from a boxing training course and was lugging a massive gym bag. As I walked into the pub, crowded and buzzing with anticipation, I swung the bag around—and promptly knocked over someone's drink.

It splashed across the bar and I turned around. "I'm so sorry—can I buy you another one?"

He looked up, smiled and said, "No, don't worry about it."

His name was Jason.

At half-time, we stepped outside for some fresh air and finally had a proper conversation. The game was intense and went to extra time. My heart was in my throat. Ultimately, AFC Wimbledon won 4–3 on penalties.

The pub exploded in celebration and somehow Jason and I were right in the middle of it—hugging, laughing, high on adrenaline and joy. After the match, my friends drifted off, but I stayed back. Jason and I spent the evening together, soaking in the magic of the win, enjoying drinks and one another's company. A most unexpected connection came over us; it was simultaneously the most ordinary and *extra*ordinary beginning to our love story.

Being with Jason felt different. He wasn't just another passing romance; he was steady, kind and he saw me—*really saw me*. When I was with him, I felt safe in a way I never had before. He made me believe in love, in family, in a future that didn't have to be dictated by my past.

When our first daughter was born, something shifted inside me. Holding her in my arms, I knew with absolute certainty: I would never let her feel the kind of pain I had felt. I would break the cycle. I would give her the childhood I had longed for.

For the first time, it felt like I was not just surviving—I was *thriving*. Building a future filled with possibilities, not fear. A life shaped by love, not shame.

It wasn't perfect. I wasn't perfect.

But for the first time, I believed: *maybe that was enough.*

The Patterns That Won't Let Go

But some things weren't so easy to escape. I had cut down on smoking weed. But drinking? That was harder to control. Most of the time, I was fine with a casual drink at the pub. But then, every once in a while, the old me would take over

—one drink became two... two became five. And then suddenly, I'd find myself back there—wild and reckless, like nothing had changed. I told myself it wasn't a problem—that I was just having fun. I didn't want to admit it, but part of me was still running, as though I couldn't trust my own happiness.

The Absurdity of It All

Over time, I had stopped thinking about my stepdad as much as I used to. I told myself it didn't matter anymore. He was old. He would die soon. And when He did, the problem would disappear with Him. Until then, I would keep pretending. Pretending our family was normal. Pretending the past didn't exist. Pretending I wasn't still carrying it all inside me.

Eventually, the time came for Jason to meet my parents. I stood there, looking on as the love of my life shook the hand of the man who had destroyed my childhood and I said nothing. I acted like everything was fine. Like this was just another family dinner. The absurdity of it all wasn't lost on me, but I had become an expert at pretending it didn't exist —no matter how suffocating or ridiculous it was. But I swallowed it down, the way I always had. Because what else could I do? Secrets had become a way of life for me.

"Is your dad going to walk you down the aisle?" my friend had asked me one day.

What an innocent and ordinary question. Dads walking their beloved daughters down the aisle—a common sight at weddings. It's a beautiful scene, as a father gives his support and blessing, ushering his daughter into the next phase of her life. I've always taken it for a deeply emotional moment that reflects a father's love and pride.

Oh dear Lord, there is no way in hell He is walking me down the aisle. I screamed within myself. This was a red line for me. It couldn't be crossed. It would be absurd to have the abuser walk me down the aisle.

How do I get out of this one?

"It seems a bit old-fashioned to me," I said. "Patriarchal even—like transferring authority over from father to husband."

Good one, I thought to myself, pleased with my own quick thinking on the spot.

Our daughter would be nine months old on our wedding day and so I had the idea that I could carry her down the aisle. With our beautiful baby girl in my arms, I'd walk down the aisle with pure, unadulterated love and joy. I could start a new tradition. I had no control over the family that I had been born into. But I could start to control the part I play in this loving family that we'd built for ourselves.

If I'd had a proper dad, of course I would have loved Him to walk me down the aisle. I could have thanked Him for everything He had done for me—for all the love, support and guidance He had bestowed on me. All those girls who are blessed with wonderful dads—I hope they know how lucky they are.

I decided that I would carry our baby down the aisle. I framed it as a modern choice, repeating my rhetoric about how it felt outdated for a father to walk his daughter. But the truth was, I was deceiving myself—it was a mask, a cover story.

A New Beginning

I'd given birth to our second daughter a year after the wedding. Her arrival felt like another new beginning, filled with small hands, sleepy cries, late-night feeds and the quiet awe of watching her tiny body grow. Life became a blur of milestones and milk-stained clothes. Having two daughters under two years old brought chaos and joy in equal measure.

There were moments, in those early years, when things almost felt... normal. Stable, even. I was building something I had never known myself: a safe family. A home rooted in love instead of fear. I was building a life my childhood self would have loved. A home filled with laughter, warmth and safety.

And then, without any warning, the unimaginable happened.

15

SMOKE AFTER FIRE

My swimming costume was too small. I tugged at the straps, twisting my body in the changing room mirror, frustrated with how tight it was around my chest. Just then—there it was.

A lump.

I froze.

It was small but firm, sitting just beneath my skin. My breathing felt tight as I pressed my fingers against it, hoping it was just some weird swelling. Something harmless, like a muscle knot.

A week later, I found myself at the breast clinic. The doctor prodded the lump, her fingers cool and clinical, her face unreadable.

"It's benign," she said, her voice reassuring. "Nothing to worry about."

A wave of relief washed over me. I went home and held

my daughters—my babies, just one and three years old—telling myself I was fine.

But then, a week later, I returned to the breast clinic to get my biopsy results. I breezed in, light-hearted, unconcerned. It all just seemed like a formality. I noticed a nurse sitting in the corner of the room. Not the doctor's assistant—a nurse.

My stomach flipped.

Why is she here?

My instinct told me this was not good. "I'm so sorry," the doctor said. "It's breast cancer."

The words didn't land at first. Not properly. A week ago, I was fine.

I stared at her, waiting for her to take it back, to tell me there had been a mistake. That they had mixed up my results with someone else's.

But no. *Cancer.* The word lingered in the air like a venomous whisper.

I nodded, numb. My body felt detached from me, as though I were watching myself from the corner of the room, hearing a doctor tell a woman she had cancer while she just sat there, blinking, frozen.

My mind raced to my daughters. *Would I see them grow up? Would I be there for their first day of school? Their teenage years and their weddings?*

I should have fallen apart. I should have taken this as the sign it was—a blaring alarm from my body, screaming at me to stop, to heal, to finally take care of myself.

But I didn't. Instead, after my first chemo session, I went home and rolled a joint.

The irony wasn't lost on me. I had breast cancer. I was fighting for my life. And yet, I was still abusing myself.

I smoked after chemo, letting the haze settle over me, as if I could escape the reality of what was happening. My body, battered by years of trauma, was breaking down and I was still refusing to listen.

Vana's Death & the Unfairness of It All

As if times weren't hard enough, Vana had died as I was undergoing chemotherapy. She had been my second mother, the woman who had loved me when my own mother couldn't. I was devastated by this loss.

When I stood up at her funeral to give the eulogy, I felt like I was standing on the edge of a cliff—grief threatening to pull me under. I spoke about her kindness, her warmth and the way she had always been my cheerleader. And then, as I looked at her coffin, something twisted deep inside me.

Why do the good ones go? Why did she die and yet He was still alive?

I didn't work for a year. I lost my hair. My children didn't understand why their mummy looked different, why I was too tired to play some days and why I spent so much time lying on the couch.

I worried constantly. *Would I survive? Would they remember me if I didn't? Would they grow up knowing how much I loved them?*

But what I didn't ask—what I *couldn't* ask—was the overarching question which summed up my life: *Why didn't I love myself enough to stop hurting myself?*

I should have known better. I should have woken up. But I didn't. Not yet.

Following six months of gruelling chemotherapy and a mastectomy on my right breast, I finally had beaten cancer. It was a fight I'd never signed up for, but it is one that I survived. I had fought for my life with everything I had. And yet, even after all that, I still wasn't fighting for myself.

I had won the battle against disease, but the psychological war was harder to win.

A Truth That Changed Nothing

The dynamic between my brother and me had seen a considerable transition as we each became parents. Maybe it was the weight of responsibility—the quiet, mutual understanding that we were now the grown-ups. That we had children of our own to protect. Maybe it was the creeping fear that history might repeat itself in ways we couldn't yet see. That silence, left unchecked, had a way of echoing forward. Either way, we knew. *It was time to tell her.*

We went to our mother's house together, the unspoken weight of this decision pressing upon us. She was surprised to see us both turn up unannounced, but she made coffee as if this were just an ordinary visit. The kitchen smelled of my mother's cooking. How could a place hold so much comfort and so much pain at the same time?

Then, the moment came.

"We need to talk," I said.

The words felt too small for what was about to happen. I glanced at my brother, bracing myself. Then, for the first time, I told my mother what her husband had done to me. What I had carried all these years. I watched her face carefully, searching for something—horror, rage, sorrow, regret. Anything.

She blinked once. Then twice. She looked... shocked. But not in the way I needed her to be. It felt like she didn't fully grasp what I was saying—or maybe, she didn't want to.

And then—nothing.

She did not leave Him. She did not demand an explanation. She did not cry or scream or hold me and say, *I am so sorry this happened to you.* She just kept going about her—business as usual. She still cooked for Him. She still washed his underpants.

We never revisited the topic again. We went back to eating Croatian soup at dinner, the silence thick as steam rising from the *Juha*. And just like that, the family tradition of silence resumed. *Nothing to see here. Nothing to say.*

Denial was the family glue. And once again, we stuck ourselves together with it.

16

LOCKDOWN AND THE DEATH PLAN'S FATAL FLAW

I'd maintained the facade, holding my breath—waiting for my stepfather to die—as the family carried on pretending.

Then—COVID.

The world shut down. We were in lockdown. Everything slowed. We stopped seeing people. Strangely, it was a relief.

I didn't have to go to family gatherings, didn't have to sit across from Him at the dinner table pretending everything was fine. I could breathe.

Or at least, I thought I could. But in the stillness, something I had been running from became painfully clear. I had built my life around the assumption that his death would set me free. But He wasn't dying. And I had no backup plan.

For years, I had convinced myself that I didn't need to act because, sooner or later, nature would take care of it for me. I wouldn't have to be the one to rip the family apart. I wouldn't have to say the words out loud. I wouldn't have to acknowledge the absurdity of the situation—that I had spent my entire adult life pretending a man who destroyed me was just any ordinary dad.

But being locked in my home with nothing but my own thoughts, I began to see things clearly.

Waiting for his death wasn't a plan. It was avoidance. And if I didn't take control of my own life—if I didn't stop waiting—I would be trapped forever.

Maybe It Was Time to Tell My Husband

Seventeen years had passed since I first remembered my childhood abuse. And I had never told anyone outside of mental health professionals and my family of origin.

Until now.

The day I decided to tell him, my husband was working from home. I thought I would wait until he finished work and tell him then. I would be brave.

When the moment had come, I knew it was time to face life head on, no matter how difficult it would be.

I could hear him on the phone, meeting after meeting. *Is he ever going to finish?*

Emotions bubbled around me as my anxiety skyrocketed and the hours dragged on.

Finally, he finished working.

"Can I talk to you about something?"

"Can it wait? I need to get some fresh air."

"Okay," I said, swallowing my nerves. *Eek.*

"When will you be back?"

"I won't be long."

Breathe. Just breathe. He'll be back soon. Where is he? Why has he gone for such a long walk?

I tried to meditate, then started praying.

Help me, God. Please help me. I really need some extra strength right now.

Finally, the door opened. My husband was home.

"Can we talk now?"

"Yeah, sure," he said casually, taking his coat off.

"Before I tell you, I just need you to understand how hard this has been for me."

He studied my face.

"Are you having an affair?"

"Gosh, no! I would never do that," I replied quickly.

Admitting to an affair might have been easier—I could have pleaded for mercy, begged for forgiveness. But somehow, this felt worse.

I had kept such a significant part of my life hidden, intending to take it to the grave. Yet, of course, my stepfather couldn't just die. I was furious that He hadn't. That He hadn't set me free.

I forced myself to meet my husband's eyes. My throat tightened.

Just say it. *Say it.*

"My dad abused me when I was a child."

The words left my lips and hung there, suspended in the silence between us.

For a moment, he just stared.

His face paled. He blinked, as if trying to make sense of the sentence.

As if the words were in a language he didn't quite understand.

A long, heavy beat passed.

The walls around me felt too close, the air thick.

Had I imagined this moment would bring relief? It didn't. Instead, it cracked open something raw inside me. There was no going back now.

Finally, he moved.

He gave me a hug, holding me tighter than usual.

"Why didn't you tell me when we had the children?" he asked, his voice thick with something I couldn't quite name.

Quickly, his sympathy turned to anger.

"Why haven't you done anything? You need to get justice."

His emotions were a whirlwind—anger, disbelief, sympathy, rage and disgust. His clarity was piercing.

"This is wrong."

He later accused the family of a cover-up—he had a point. We were all protecting a pedophile. We were bottled in shame and denial, heads buried in the sand.

Jason's stance was clear: *I had to do something.*

Now, the genie was out of the bottle. And all hell was about to break loose. This marked the end of my life in the sexual abuse closet and the beginning of my journey into healing.

Breaking the Silence, Breaking the Cycle

Secrets had shaped so many decisions in my life—who I trusted, what I spoke about, even how I saw myself. But for the first time, there were no more secrets. At least, not between my husband and me.

Telling him was supposed to be the hardest part. And in some ways, it was. But what I hadn't realised was that the moment I spoke the truth, I set something in motion that couldn't be undone.

For seventeen years, I had lived in a fragile world of cognitive dissonance, simultaneously championing others and hurting myself. Pretending, ignoring, just hoping He would die and take the truth with him.

But now, I could no longer pretend. Not to myself, not to my husband. And, eventually, not to the world.

Jason was clear.

"You have to do something."

His words rang in my ears long after the conversation ended. My heart pounded whenever I thought about it. But the idea of stepping forward, of taking action, filled me with something I hadn't expected: fear.

What if people don't believe me? What if my family turns against me? What if this destroys everything?

I wanted justice. But I wanted peace even more. I wasn't sure if those two desires could coexist.

For weeks, I sat with this impossible choice. Until the phone rang.

"We need to inform you—your father has confessed."

I felt my chest grow tighter. It was the police.

Confessed? My mind spun. *Did I hear that right?*

Yes. He had confessed. Fully. Completely. No denial. No minimisation. He told them exactly what He had done to me. But why?

The Pressure That Made Him Crack

He hadn't confessed out of guilt, nor out of remorse. He confessed because He had no choice. Jason had given Him an ultimatum.

"You go to the police—or I will."

He must have known Jason wasn't bluffing.

This wasn't just a private family reckoning anymore—Jason wasn't playing by the old family rules. He was ready to make this public

My stepfather was faced with two options: Either He could go to the police and control the narrative, or Jason would do it for him and He'd lose all control.

And so, for the first time in his life, my stepfather faced the music and admitted the truth.

Not because He was brave. Not because He was sorry. But because He was afraid. Afraid of losing control. Afraid of Jason. Afraid that this time, He wouldn't be able to twist the story in his favour. So, He walked into a police station, sat down and confessed. Decades after the abuse, He finally spoke the words out loud that revealed his heinous crimes.

Now, the decision was in my hands. Would I want to proceed with prosecution?

17

THE COURTROOM SCENE

The decision to prosecute is never a simple one. It's a delicate algebra of pain, healing and justice—each variable weighted with personal history and previously unspoken trauma.

From the age of seven to seventeen, my childhood was systematically stolen from me. I'd been thrown into a futile decade of silence and survival. Each year layered another sediment of trauma, replacing my innocence and growth with a landscape of relentless violation.

And so, I was faced with a choice.

Jason's intervention had been pivotal. By delivering that ultimatum—"Go to the police, or I will"—he had forced something I never thought possible. He made a man who had hidden in the shadows for decades finally step into the light.

But the weight of that decision still sat with me. I felt conflicted. He was an old man—frail, diminished, well into his late 80s. The monster of my childhood had become a shadow of himself. I couldn't ignore the discomfort of sending an old man to prison. Against all reason, I felt compassion for Him, however unwarranted.

Brighton Beach and the Inner Child's Answer

I walked along Brighton Beach, the wind cold against my face, the stones shifting beneath my feet.

I wasn't alone.

I was with Her—the little girl who had hidden inside me for so long. The child who had spent years keeping secrets too heavy for her small body to carry.

I had made Her a promise during my therapeutic journey. We will make decisions together from now on. You will never be alone again. And so, I asked Her: *What do you need?*

She didn't want revenge. She didn't want to see Him suffer. She wanted to be heard. She wanted to be acknowledged. She wanted to exist in a world where someone finally said: *What happened to you was wrong.*

I closed my eyes, feeling the wind whip my hair, the waves crash in front of me. We made the decision together. We would go ahead with the prosecution.

Beyond the Courtroom: A Different Kind of Justice

The practical realities of prosecution weighed on me heavily.

I knew the statistics; most sexual abuse cases never see a conviction. Survivors frequently encounter institutional indifference, re-traumatisation and legal labyrinths designed to obscure rather than illuminate truth. As He had confessed, I would be spared a trial—I was one of the "lucky ones."

But this wasn't about winning a legal battle. This was about transforming personal pain into collective healing. When asked if I wanted to read my victim impact statement, I said yes. After years of silence, I would finally speak. I would stand in court and tell my story, not for revenge but for healing. For the little girl who loved hymns and needed protection.

For every child who carries secrets too heavy to bear.
For the child I was.
For the woman I became.
For all those still searching for their own path to healing.
Because, in the end, the greatest act of justice was choosing voice over silence.

A Signpost Named Simon

The months leading up to the court date had been a blur of anxiety, fear and the slow unraveling of a life built on silence. I was standing on the edge of something terrifying—exposing the truth in a way I never had before. And then, just before that reckoning, the universe sent me a message.

His name was Simon.

I was covering a yoga class at the same studio where I'd first practised years earlier—rounding this out as one of those full-circle moments life hands you when you least expect it.

After class, as I stacked mats, a man approached me.

"Great session," he said, his voice steady, warm. We fell into easy conversation—the kind that flows without effort. We'd covered books, ideas and healing. We talked about the kind of books that don't just teach, but transform. (*The Body Keeps the Score, The Untethered Soul* and authors like *Thich Nhat Hanh*.)

And then he said it, simply, quietly: "I was sexually abused as a child."

No hesitation. No shame. Just a truth laid bare, as casually as if he'd said, "I used to play the piano."

Something inside me stilled. At that point, only a few people knew my story. I had spent years layering it with silence, distraction and shame. Yet here was someone speaking it aloud—no shame, no caution. Just telling his truth.

My gut said I could trust him. "Me too," I said before I had time to second-guess myself.

He didn't flinch. No awkward pause, no pity. Just understanding. A quiet, invisible thread stitched between us.

"I'm Simon, by the way."

"Hi, Simon. Lovely to meet you."

And I meant it.

Simon became a signpost on my path to healing. His ease around disclosure planted something in me—a thought I hadn't dared to entertain: *What if this shame was never mine to carry?*

Later, he told me he'd felt a pull to stay and talk. A quiet knowing that our meeting was meant to happen. I believe that too. The universe moves in mysterious ways, gently nudging us toward people who will change us.

Because there he was, standing in his truth—while I was still learning how to stand in mine.

That conversation planted a seed. But I wasn't ready to act on it yet. I kept moving forward, bracing for the storm ahead. The day I walked into the courtroom, I wasn't thinking about healing. I was just trying to survive.

But something about meeting Simon stayed with me. His calm, his openness, the way he carried his story without shame—it stirred something deep inside me. I'd become inspired. A quiet thought began to form, not from anything he said, but from the space he held.

Maybe I didn't have to carry this shame after all.

Something inside me had begun to shift.

As the court date approached, I realised I wasn't just preparing to stand before a judge—I was preparing to finally stand in my own truth.

Court

The day of the court case arrived. My inner child and I held hands. We were ready. This was our chance to tell our story. We would stand up in court and read our victim impact statement. The police officer dealing with the case was on annual leave, so there would be no one we knew in the court apart from our abuser. I guess it was just me and my inner child.

I had declined an offer of an ISVA (Independent Sexual Violence Advisor). I wondered if acronyms offered a false sense of security? I felt it was just one more thing to have to remember, to worry about. In hindsight, it would have been great to have had that support. I wasn't used to having people support me, so I had decided to go it alone. I have since learnt to lean on people and let them support me when needed. My advice to anyone going through the legal system is to grab all the support that's available. It is a very clinical process. So it is integral that you find an advisor that you connect with; they will provide practical and emotional support and ensuring your needs are respected throughout the legal process, which can feel cold and intimidating.

I took the train to Kingston Magistrates Court, avoiding buses. I was nervous that my stepfather might take the bus. I didn't want to see Him, to sit there imagining what was going through his mind. And perhaps it would be his last bus journey as a free man. Was He feeling any remorse? Was He scared? He had avoided punishment for decades. He had silenced me. The statistics said that if He had lived to the average age of a man in the UK, in his situation, He ought to be dead by now. His longevity was a sort of curse and it meant that at the age of 89, He was finally being held accountable. He'd probably survive to 100 with my perpetual bad luck. Would that even set me free? It might have made things easier for *Him*, but what about *me*?

It was a September afternoon when I caught that train to Kingston. Queen Elizabeth had died that month at the ripe old age of 96. Death would have been his easy escape, but in that moment, He was forced to face his crimes. If he had just died, then I wouldn't be on this train—I wouldn't have to deal with all this. The problem would be gone. I know now that his death would not have set me free. Justice is elusive and changes its shape when you try to touch it. I suppose I *am* one of the "lucky" ones. My abuser would become publicly and officially culpable for his crimes.

I tossed and turned the night before. I'd kept trying to coax myself back to sleep, as I wanted to be well rested. Lying in bed in the middle of the night worrying would not serve me well.

I arrived at the court and met the prosecutor for the first time. We sat in a featureless room which might as well have been in any public building. "Your police statement was very powerful," she said. She warned me that I would hear details in the courtroom about the abuse. Apparently the judge would "try to keep this to a minimum as you are present."

My mind went back to the police interview. I'd had to give so much detail. All the things He had done to me. Often difficult to put into words. One of the most painful memories was when I wasn't allowed to sleep at a friend's house because I was "naughty." That night He abused me. He acted like it was some sort of justice. Like abusing me was the right thing to do. But it was his twisted self-interest that took a ten-year-old from that sleepover. Did He have an urge that just had to be scratched? An usher took me up into the courtroom. Just before entering, I asked if I could take a breath. I was very nervous but managed to steady myself. We entered the courtroom. I saw my stepfather in the dock. I'd avoided eye contact with Him and took a seat next to the usher. I resisted the urge to look at his face. The details of the abuse were shared with the court. It all sounded very clinical. The lawyer linked the crimes to particular points in my growing up.

The time came to read my victim impact statement. The judge asked me if I wanted to read it out where I was, facing

Him, with my dad behind me. I am using the term 'dad' here as He *was* my dad. All my childhood He was my dad. Only in my 30s did I learn we shared no blood—another layer of betrayal. A father's love is sacred; He was my betrayer instead. He beat me for stealing a hymn book and filled my childhood with nightmares.

I stood up and read my statement, deliberately reminding myself of the wisdom of the word "mindfulness." *Breathe.* This is finally our moment to be heard. My voice was shaky, but I managed to project so I could be heard. I held back tears as I read my victim impact statement. I could feel the people in the courtroom affected by my words. I glanced at the usher next to me and could see tears in her eyes.

I finished reading. The courtroom was silent, the weight of my words still hanging in the air. I had taken my power back.

He shrank to he—Him to him.

I kept my gaze forward, he was my past; I was done looking back.

It's easy to ask, 'Why didn't she say something sooner?'

Harder to understand what it costs to lose a family you've spent your life trying to protect—even from the truth.

The judge thanked me for being so brave. "Not many people are able to read out their statements. It made a great impact coming directly from you."

He was sentenced to twelve years in prison. Nine, with the reduction for his guilty plea.

There was no rush of relief, no sense of triumph. Just a quiet, heavy exhaustion. The kind that settles in your bones.

I glanced around the courtroom. There was no applause,

no moment of celebration. Just silence. Justice, it turns out, wasn't the sharp, clean thing I thought it would be. It wasn't a 9 o'clock courtroom TV drama. It was messy. Hollow. Necessary, but not enough.

The prosecutor hugged me afterward in the same bare room we'd sat in earlier. "You were incredibly brave," she said. I nodded, but I didn't feel brave. I just felt… sad. Like I had finally set something down, but I wasn't sure if it was enough to make me feel whole again.

Then came the hardest part.

18

NOT OUR SHAME

I got the bus to my mother's house. I knew I wouldn't have to worry about bumping into him again—he wouldn't be traveling on a bus again, maybe ever. That thought should have brought comfort, but all I felt was numbness.

The court had planned to call her, but I knew the news should come from me. So I walked up to her door, stomach twisted in knots, hoping—maybe, somehow—she would finally *see* me. I had called my brother to tell him what had happened and by the time I got to my mum's, she already knew about the verdict.

When she opened the door and saw me standing there, her face darkened. And then, without a word, she slammed the door in my face.

I stood there, stunned. After everything, after all these years, this was still her reaction. Not anger at him. Not concern for me. Just... rejection.

My brother let me in. She sat in the living room with her arms folded, silent. I asked her the question I had wanted to ask for years.

"Why didn't you leave him?" My voice was steady, but my hands shook. "You knew what he did to me and you stayed."

She didn't meet my eyes. She just stared at the floor, lips pressed into a thin line. I thought she wouldn't answer, but then, in a whisper, she said: "He is my husband."

How do you survive a betrayal that begins at home? My mother—who wasn't just a bystander, but a complex mix of survival and silence—had made choices that fractured me, yet kept me alive.

When my biological father abandoned us, she didn't discard me. Her silence perhaps wasn't weakness—it was a strategy of endurance. Survival sometimes looks like compliance and sounds like silence.

Generations of women before her had learnt this brutal truth—protect what little you have, even if the cost is your child's innocence. Maybe the byproduct of her cognitive dissonance wasn't cruelty, but a survival mechanism carved from generations of unspoken pain? Had she thought that speaking would destroy everything—her marriage, her security, her very existence?

In that moment, looking at her pressed-lip silence, I saw not just my mother, but every silenced woman who came before her. Was their trauma inheritance passed down like a genetic memory? And for the first time, instead of anger, I felt something deeper: a profound, aching compassion.

I took a deep breath and said, "This is not our shame."

She looked up at me then, just for a moment and for the

first time, I saw something flicker across her face; recognition, maybe even regret. Then, quietly, she said: "I know."

It wasn't an apology. It wasn't enough. But at that moment, it was something. A small crack in the wall. A glimmer of hope.

I walked out of that house—the house of my childhood, the house where I was hurt, the house where I had waited for her to save me—and I would not hear from my mum for six months. I also left with a determination to break generational trauma.

That night, I lay in bed, staring at the ceiling. The trial was over. The sentence had been handed down. The world had shifted, but inside, I still felt the same. The shame wasn't mine anymore—I knew that now. But healing wasn't about a single moment of justice. It was about every moment that came after.

I whispered to myself, "We did it. We were so brave. We went to the courtroom alone and stood up together." The sad, wounded child was part of me and together we would continue our journey.

Weeks later, I remembered the feeling of walking out of the courtroom, justice like a weight in my hands. He had been sentenced. The system had spoken. The man who had stolen my childhood would now sit behind bars. And yet there was no grand feeling of relief. No sudden lightness. The truth is that justice and healing aren't the same thing.

The court had done what it could, but it couldn't rewrite my past. It couldn't take away the nightmares, the years lost in self-destruction, the way his face appeared in my mind. It couldn't hand me back my self-worth or stitch together the parts of me that had been torn apart as a child. That was work only I could do.

And that's when I realised, justice alone wasn't going to set me free. I had to set myself free. For years, I had lived in the shadow of what happened to me. I had built my identity around the pain, around the story of survival. And don't get me wrong—there was no shame in acknowledging that I had been a victim. Because I was. A child who was betrayed, a teenager who was gaslit, an adult who carried the wounds.

But I didn't want to stay there. I was so much more than what had happened to me.

19

THE WEIGHT OF WHAT WASN'T SAID

Telling my story in court was one thing. But learning that people had suspected all along? That was a different kind of betrayal.

When I finally told a family friend what my stepfather had done to me, I braced myself for the impact. I expected shock, horror—some kind of explosion. A revelation that would shake the ground beneath them as it had once shattered mine.

Instead, there was a pause. A long, heavy pause. Then, the words I never expected arrived:

"I always thought something was off about him."

I blinked. "What?"

They hesitated, looking down. "Well... there were things that didn't seem right. But I didn't know for sure. And you never said anything..."

A cold wave of disbelief crashed over me. People had suspected. People had seen the warning signs. And yet—no one had done anything. No one had asked. No one had investigated. No one had risked being wrong in order to be right.

It deserved a scream, a shout, something loud enough to tear the sky open. But all I could do was stand there, breaking quietly inside.

Instead, a deeper sadness settled in—the kind that comes with understanding too much. Because I knew why they had stayed silent. Fear. Doubt. The discomfort of confronting something so monstrous. The hope that maybe, just maybe, they were wrong.

I understood all of it. But understanding didn't make it hurt any less. Their silence had cost me a childhood. Their inaction had given him more time, more opportunities, more years to keep destroying me in the dark.

I had spent my whole life believing that no one knew. That no one saw. That I was alone in this nightmare. But now I knew the truth: some people had their suspicions. And they had done nothing.

I don't blame them—not entirely. I know how hard it is to acknowledge something you can't prove. I know how easy it is to assume someone else will step in. But their silence was not neutral. It was a choice. And that choice had consequences.

It wasn't just strangers who stayed silent. It was people I trusted. People I loved. People who loved me. Even good people can look away when the truth feels too unbearable to face. Even the ones who should have protected me didn't know how—or didn't dare.

Their silence wasn't because they didn't care. It was because speaking the truth out loud felt too dangerous, too shameful, too taboo. But that didn't protect me. It only protected him.

One of the hardest realisations came when I found out that Vana—my second mum—had also suspected. She had taken me to see the priest for the sacrament of healing when I had my breakdown. I was drowning in shame, barely able to speak the truth to myself, let alone anyone else. And all that time, she had known something wasn't right. That knowledge weighs heavily. Why hadn't she taken me to one side? Why hadn't she looked me in the eyes and gently asked what was going on? Part of me aches at the thought. Maybe I would have told her.

If just one person had asked the right question... If just one person had risked being wrong... Maybe my story would have been different. But no one did. And so, for ten long years, I suffered in silence. And then I suffered some more.

I had spent so much of my life waiting. Waiting for someone to see. Waiting for someone to save me. Waiting for the truth to matter. But no one had.

And yet, despite everything—despite the betrayals, despite the silence, despite knowing better—a part of me still longed for someone to step forward. To right the wrongs. To say the words I had waited decades to hear: *I'm so sorry. This should never have happened to you.*

I used to think silence was the absence of care. Now I know it's often the presence of fear. But knowing that doesn't erase the ache of being unspoken for. I don't write this to point fingers. I write this to name what happened—to give voice to what was once concealed and to acknowledge the steep cost of silence

I no longer wait for someone else to speak the truth. I carry both the pain of what wasn't said—and the strength to do things differently now.

It took me 27 years to fully come out of the sexual abuse closet. The decade of abuse ended when I was 17. For the next ten years, the memories vanished into the deepest recesses of my mind, not by conscious choice, but as a survival instinct. It was as if my mind had locked them away and thrown away the key, protecting me in the only way it knew how.

From the moment the memories returned to the moment I finally told Jason, my husband and my safe place, the person I had built a life with, another 17 years passed. That was the moment I fully owned it out loud. Not just in therapy. Not just in quiet disclosures to my family of origin. But in love, in partnership and in the open.

Simon, who has supported many survivors, often says that it takes an average of 28 years to come out of the sexual abuse closet. When I first heard that, it stopped me in my tracks because that was almost exactly my timeline too.

Trauma silences. Shame buries. And society still makes it painfully hard to tell the truth about abuse. But when we do, something shifts. A door opens. The healing begins.

20

HOPE, FANTASY AND THE TRUTH

Six months passed before my mother finally called me.

Her voice was the same—steady, familiar. But I noticed the absence of what I longed to hear most. There was no apology. No acknowledgement. Just the same old rhythm of conversation we always fell into, pretending the past didn't exist. We stuck our heads in the sand, just like always. Still, hope was a stubborn thing. It clung to me, whispering that maybe, just maybe, this time would be different.

I told Jason she had called. He listened quietly, then said, "Before the girls see her again, I want to speak to her myself."

His words shouldn't have made me nervous, but they did. I knew Jason wasn't afraid of confrontation. He wouldn't tiptoe around things like I did. He would demand the truth. And the truth was dangerous—what if I wasn't ready to face it?

It had been six months since my mother had spoken to me.

And in my heart, I still clung to a desperate hope: that one day, the phone would ring and she would say the words I needed to hear. That she would finally see me. That she would finally be sorry.

In my mind, I imagined it would happen like this:

The phone rings.

"Hello, darling," she would say.

I'd go to see her.

She'd open the door, her face crumpling with emotion the moment she saw me.

Tears would fill her eyes as she reached for my hands, holding them so tightly I'd think she'd never let go.

"I am so sorry, darling," she'd whisper.

"I am so sorry I didn't protect you."

Her voice would tremble, thick with grief. Her whole body would be shaking. "I had no idea he was doing those things to you," she'd say, with horror in her voice. "How did this happen without me noticing? How could he do this to you—to our family?"

Her hands would cover her mouth as the sobs overtook her.

"He was a former priest, for goodness' sake. How could he do something so evil and wrong? I don't know what to say."

She'd break down completely.

"I will do everything I can to support you. I'll do everything I can to make this better. Gosh, you must have felt so alone and scared."

Her grip on my hands would tighten.

"Oh, darling, I wish you had said something to me at the time. I would have thrown him out straight away."

She'd pull me into her arms, rocking me like I was a child again.

"We will get through this together," she'd promise.

"We are a family."

"You're not alone."

"I love you so much."

And then, finally—

"I am so, so sorry."

She'd bury her face in my shoulder, her grief pouring out in waves.

"I'm so sorry you couldn't talk to me. Maybe I was too busy working. Maybe I didn't give you enough attention. If I had, maybe you could have told me."

She'd shake her head in anguish.

"How could I not have seen anything? We lived in a small house! Did he do it when I was at work? Oh no... what about those times I went to Croatia—leaving you alone with him?"

Her hands would fly to her face.

"Oh, God. Did he do it then?"

Her voice would crack with devastation.

"How could he do this? He is a monster."

In my imagination, for the first time in my life, I felt seen and held.

Maybe now, things could be different. Maybe we could heal together. Maybe now, we could finally be a family. I allow myself this brief fantasy of a mother who acknowledges my pain. But none of it happened. The silence returned, heavier than ever before.

~

THE APOLOGY I'd longed for never arrived. If it had, it might have softened the wound. But instead, my mother continued to say nothing. She didn't comfort me, didn't acknowledge my pain, didn't tell me she was sorry. She talked about herself. How *she* felt. How hard this was for *her*. How *she* was struggling with the shame of it all.

I had waited my whole life for her to stand up for me. And when the moment came, she chose herself instead. Had she been blind to what was happening? Or had she turned a blind eye? If I had believed she knew and did nothing, I would have walked away and never looked back. But she told me she didn't know. So I had to take her at her word. But even now—with him gone—she still wasn't acting like the mother I needed her to be. She used to call me *Guska*—goose in English. Was it affectionate teasing or something mean-spirited? It had always felt like a scold more often than not. I never felt the love I craved.

Still, I kept going back. Hoping. Hoping that this time she would see me. That this time she would say, *"I am so sorry for what you've been through."* That this time she would love me the way I had always needed her to.

But she never did.

~

ONE DAY, my husband and I went to see her.

Jason was clear. He wanted to see her stand up for me.

"Choose your daughter over him," he said.

She hesitated.

Jason, exasperated, went outside to get something from the car. In that moment, I made a choice. When he returned, I lied. I told him, *"She chose me."*

She hadn't. She had said nothing. But I had been the peacemaker all my life. I had spent years patching up wounds, smoothing over cracks, trying to make the family whole—at my own cost. So I told myself it was true. That she had chosen me. That the words I had needed to hear had actually been spoken. But it was like putting a plaster on a broken leg. It wouldn't hold. It couldn't.

21

CHOOSING MYSELF

Healing, I've learnt, is not linear. Instead of stepping fully into the light, I hovered on the edges—one foot in survival, the other tangled in self-destruction. I told myself I was fine. Functional. Not like *those* people. But deep down, I knew better. The patterns were still there. Waiting. And then came the night I could no longer lie to myself. The night I hit a wall so hard that pretending was no longer an option.

It was July 31st, 2021: the night that became known as the vomit dress incident. At one of our first post-pandemic gatherings, I started drinking in the afternoon—glass after glass of Pimm's, unaware (or perhaps choosing not to care) that it contained wine. When the Pimm's ran out, I moved on to cocktails. Sex on the Beach, Blue Lagoon and Woo Woo were my drinks of choice on this occasion.

The Queen tribute band played, as I stumbled across the

garden, eventually toppling onto my daughter during a particularly enthusiastic rendition of "Don't Stop Me Now."

The taxi ride home became my moment of reckoning. One moment I was swaying in the front seat, the next I was watching horror spread across my children's faces as vomit splattered across my dress and the car's interior. The driver erupted, ordering us all out—my mortified husband, my terrified children and me: their wreck of a wife and mother.

Lying on the hard South London pavement, I felt the weight of my daughters' eyes on me. Their confusion and fear cut deeper than any hangover ever could.

The next morning, sprawled on a friend's couch in that same vomit-stained dress, I had one of the worst hangovers of my life. I remembered my husband shaking me the night before, his voice strained: "Pull yourself together, woman."

He had never called me "woman" before. Hearing it from him—gentle, steady Jason—felt like a slap. He must have been at his wits' end.

That was it. The line in the sand. Not a gentle nudge or a flexible boundary—an absolute. I would never drink again.

This time, it wasn't just about me. It was about my children having the mother they deserved.

I was 45 years old and had spent a lifetime running. But here, in yesterday's dress, I knew: this was not who I wanted to be. Not anymore. My decision to quit drinking wasn't a reaction. It wasn't an escape. It was the first real choice I had made in a long time.

Prior to this, everything had been about survival—numbing, running, pretending. Drinking had been a crutch, a mask, a way to quiet the chaos inside of me. But in that moment, having my children's frightened faces burned into my mind's eye, something clicked.

This wasn't just about stopping. It was about reclaiming. Reclaiming my body. My choices. My life. For the first time, I wasn't making a decision based on fear or shame. I wasn't just trying to erase the past or outrun the pain. I was choosing something different. I was choosing me. And after all these years, I was beginning to heal.

But giving up alcohol was just one piece of the puzzle. The real work, the harder work, was facing the pain I had buried for decades. Because the chaos inside me didn't start with Pimm's and cocktails. It started with silence. With the ache of not being protected. With a mother who couldn't, or wouldn't see me. If quitting drinking was the moment I chose my children, what came next was the moment I finally chose myself.

The last time I went to my mother's house, something inside me snapped. The rage I had swallowed for decades finally erupted—rage that had lived inside me like a quiet, festering wound, buried beneath layers of forced politeness and a desperate hope that, somehow, things could still be salvaged. But that day, there was no more swallowing it down. No more pretending.

I started punching the walls.

Fist after fist, the pain registering somewhere beneath the sheer force of my emotions but not enough to stop me. Not enough to silence the years of screaming inside my head. "Do you have any idea what I've been through?" I screamed, my voice raw, torn open.

I was screaming—at him, at her, at myself, at the years

lost, at the life stolen from me. At the times I had protected them when no one had protected me. At the ways I had begged for scraps of love, of validation, of acknowledgment —and received breadcrumbs.

And I was screaming at myself.

For the self-betrayal. For making myself small. For walking across the bridge a thousand times, hoping that one day, she would take a single step toward me.

Finally, after all these years, I saw some emotion from my mother. She began to cry. But even then, she still didn't say she was sorry.

Her face was streaked with tears, but her lips remained pressed together, unwilling or unable to say the words I needed to hear. Maybe she was crying for me. Maybe she was crying for herself. Maybe she was crying because she was scared.

I didn't know. And in that moment, I stopped trying to understand her silence.

I looked down. My knuckles throbbed, raw and red, blood trickling down my fingers.

I had hurt myself. Again. The realisation cut through the rage like a knife.

How many times had I done this —inflicted pain on myself in the name of keeping the peace? Swallowed my feelings, smiled through the discomfort, bent myself into a version that she could tolerate, all at the expense of my own soul? How many times had I placed my well-being below everyone else's?

I was done.

That's when I saw it.

A photograph.

The picture on the cover of this book.

It had been sitting there for years, unnoticed, like a ghost of the past, waiting for me to find it. I picked it up with shaking hands, my breath catching as I took in the image—me. A child. Innocent. Unaware of what was to come. A little girl, wearing the glasses she hated, in school uniform. I had spent my entire life trying to be seen. And here I was, looking at a version of myself that had been waiting to be rescued all along.

I had to get her out.

I picked up the picture and whispered, "You're coming with me. I'm going to save you." It was symbolic. I couldn't save my mother. I couldn't change the past. But I could save myself.

I gently placed the photo in my bag and took her home with me. In that photograph, I finally saw clearly—the child that had always needed someone else to rescue. But nobody ever did. Now, it was my turn. I would rescue the child.

As I closed the door on the hope of a traditional mother-daughter relationship, I began to open doors within myself that I never thought I could. Letting go of the expectation that my mother would change, that she would apologise or validate my pain, was one of the hardest things I had ever done. But it was also one of the most freeing. I had spent a lifetime trying to force a connection that wasn't meant to be, pushing my own needs aside in hopes of something that would never come.

In walking away, I wasn't abandoning my mother—I was choosing myself. For the first time, I was listening to my inner child, acknowledging her pain and giving her the love and protection she had always needed. I began to heal, not by waiting for someone else to make it right, but by taking responsibility to nurture myself. This wasn't an easy journey, but it was necessary.

I would never be born into the family of my dreams; the one where love, support and safety were constants. But I could create a new family—one based on chosen connections, on mutual respect, love and healing. I could be the parent to my inner child that I never had and in doing so, I could begin to repair the wounds that had been buried for so long.

The road ahead is not without its struggles, but it is mine to walk. I am not defined by the past or by the people who failed to protect me. I am defined by my strength, my resilience and my commitment to healing.

Though I may never receive the validation I longed for, I no longer need it. The power to heal was always in my hands and I am learning to trust that power each day.

22

VICTIM BLAMING AND DISCLOSURE

Simon, who I had met a year before the court case, had become a good friend. He often spoke about Survivors UK, a charity dedicated to supporting men, boys and non-binary individuals who had experienced sexual violence. He had found connection there, a place where he wasn't alone in his pain. It made me wonder—could I find that too? Could I allow myself to be seen, truly seen, by others who understood?

After some searching, I found Survivors Together, a support group in East London that offered both online and in-person meetings.

I'll never forget my first session, which took place just before Christmas. We sat together making Christmas cards —a simple activity, but in that moment, it became something deeper. The act of creation, of crafting something tangible with my hands, mirrored the slow, deliberate work of rebuilding myself. There was something profoundly healing about being in a room with others who got it. No explanations were needed; the unspoken understanding between us created a sanctuary of safety and acceptance.

In personal conversations, healing begins. Within a safe space, we can share our pain, speak our truths and be fully present for one another. "I am deeply sorry you have experienced a similar journey. Thank you for sharing your story and know that if you wish to talk again, I am here to listen." The words exchanged in that room weren't just words—they were lifelines. Others on similar paths knew the depth of this pain, the way betrayal wounds deeper than the body, how shame keeps us silent. Yet, the more we spoke, the more we released its grip.

I realised then—I deserved this. I deserved a place where I was understood. To be heard by those who had walked this road. Healing didn't have to be a solitary process. Sometimes, it is in witnessing each other's pain, in holding space for one another, that we find our own strength.

The more I allowed myself to be vulnerable in spaces like Survivors Together, the more I began to see the stark contrast between true support and the reactions I had encountered elsewhere. In that room, I didn't have to defend myself, justify my feelings, or fight to be believed. But outside, in the real world, disclosure was never that simple. I had started to trust that healing was possible, that people could hold space for my pain—but what about those who couldn't?

When I imagined telling my friend Helen about my childhood abuse, I pictured warmth and empathy: "Daniela, I'm so sorry for what happened to you. If there's anything I can do to support you, please let me know," she'd say, pulling me into a hug. "You are loved and worthy." But that's not what happened.

Instead, her words landed strangely, like a note played out of tune. At first, I wasn't sure I had heard her correctly. "Do you remember when we were children and your mum would have a go at you and you said nothing? Maybe if you weren't so passive, you would've spoken up back then.

I blinked. *Huh?* My mind tried to make sense of it, to twist her words into something that wasn't cruel. But she kept going, relentlessly.

"And how could you have done this to your mum?"

A dull roar filled my ears. The familiar hurt welled up inside me, bubbling to the surface like an old wound being ripped open.

Was she blaming me?

I had been so excited to see Helen—my friend since childhood. As children we'd spent hours watching cartoons together, giggling, scribbling in our notebooks. But now? Now, I couldn't recognise the person sitting across from me.

Why didn't I tell anyone during my childhood? That question has haunted me for years. If I had told a trusted adult, could I have been saved? But it was the 1980s. Childhood abuse was rife, safeguarding policies were non-existent and children were told to obey adults without question. Kids weren't valued—they were seen, not heard. OK—I may be projecting my own childhood but that is how I feel.

Helen's words hit like a slap in the face. I wasn't passive because I wanted to be. I was seven years old. Groomed. Manipulated into silence. The adult had all the power—

using threats, money and sweets. He told me the family would break apart if I said anything.

Why did I have to explain this? Why couldn't she see it wasn't my fault?

A wave of protectiveness surged through me—for my inner child, for the little girl who had been abandoned in silence for too long.

"Get out," I said, my voice steady.

Helen stared at me, startled.

"I was a child. I was seven years old."

She opened her mouth to respond, but I wouldn't listen. "Leave. Now."

For the first time, I stood up for myself—and for Little Daniela.

As she walked out, tears streamed down my face. Through the sobs, I spoke to my inner child. *I'm so sorry you had to hear that, my love. But I'm here now. I'll protect you. No one will treat us like that again.*

I placed a hand on my heart, cradling her in my mind. *Little Daniela, I've got you. You're safe now. This isn't our shame. It never was.*

That summer, a year after the court case, I went to Croatia on holiday. I had hoped it would be a fresh start—a chance to reset, to breathe, to begin again. Instead, it turned out to be what Richard Schwartz in *No Bad Parts* calls an "AFGO"—Another F***ing Growth Opportunity. (I'll share more about Internal Family Systems and how it helped me in the second half of this book.)

One day, my aunt berated me for taking the kids on a coastal walk to the next village. "It's too far for them," she said. "They're active kids," I replied, confused by her negativity. "It was like a stroll in the park for them."

But her next words cut deeper than I expected. "This is all your fault," she snapped. "Why didn't you stop him?"

I froze. My stomach twisted. "I was a child," I whispered.

To her credit, she came to me the next day and apologised. We had a heart-to-heart, but even in that apology, there was a condition. "Please don't tell anyone," she pleaded. "To je sramota," she said. In Croatian, that means, "It's shameful."

Shame. She wanted me to sweep it under the rug, but I refused. Keeping it hidden keeps the shame alive. "This isn't my shame," I told her.

But it didn't matter. The old pattern continued. A friend of the family spread rumours, saying my stepfather was now in a home with dementia. A cover story—the truth being he was in prison. Their attempts to protect the family's image only deepened the wound.

Why do people blame the victim? I've asked myself this question over and over. Is it because confronting the truth of abuse is too uncomfortable? Is it easier to shift the blame onto the victim than face the horror of the perpetrator's actions?

People say the most absurd things in response to disclosures.

"Just don't think about it again," one friend told me, as if repressing emotions were a cure.

Repression nearly killed me.

In 2017, I was diagnosed with breast cancer. Years of pushing down emotions, internalising shame and living in survival mode had taken their toll. Telling survivors to stay silent is cruel.

Silence cost me years of my life—and almost my life itself.

Would you tell a victim of armed robbery to stay quiet? A survivor of attempted murder? Why, then, is childhood sexual abuse treated differently? Disclosure isn't just hard—it's a relational hazard.

Some friends ghosted me after I told them. One never replied to my texts again. Another, someone I'd always been there for, pulled away entirely. I had spent years listening to her struggles, but when I needed her, she disappeared. The rejection hurt deeply. At the time, my self-esteem was fragile and I searched for validation from others. Losing these friendships reinforced the belief that something was wrong with me.

But disclosure also brought connection. Some people opened up to me about their own traumas, sharing things they'd never told anyone. Those moments of shared humanity were healing.

Not all disclosure experiences were painful. Amid the landscape of rejection and misunderstanding, there were moments of profound compassion—when someone truly saw me, heard me and validated my experience.

I think of the next disclosure as the goddess—not a divine being, but a woman who offered the human compassion that had lacked in my other disclosures.

She got me a cup of herbal tea and we sat by her fireplace. It was December, a week or so before Christmas. The fire crackled softly, filling the room with warmth. The scent of cinnamon and clove lingered in the air.

When I was a teenager, I babysat her children and her son was there—someone I hadn't seen for 30 years. "You were my favourite babysitter," he told me. "I think it was because you weren't very strict and let us stay up late."

I laughed, a small, unexpected moment of lightness. Then, I told her what had happened to me. She listened. Really listened. No interruptions, no questions, just pure presence. Then she said those magical words: "I am so sorry for what happened to you."

That's all I had ever wanted. Someone to say sorry. "Is there anything I can do to help you move forward?" she asked.

She listened with compassion and love. I felt heard, seen, validated. When she hugged me goodbye, I didn't want to let go. My inner child didn't want to let go. Oh, how it could have been so different if she had been my mum.

23

THE QUESTION THAT CUT DEEP

Disclosing my truth wasn't just about seeking understanding—it was about testing the waters of truth. Each time I spoke, I hoped for compassion, for someone to hold my pain with me. Sometimes, I found it. Other times, I faced something much colder: judgment, discomfort and even blame. I had expected that from strangers, from those who didn't know better. But when it came from those I loved, from people I thought were safe—it cut differently. It forced me to confront the deeper wounds I had been avoiding, the ones that whispered: *Was it my fault? Could I have done something to stop it?*

And then, one question left a mark I couldn't ignore.

The Question That Cut Deep

I almost left this part out of the book. Even now, as I write these words, I feel a tightness in my chest—a deep discomfort that tempts me to press delete. But I refuse to let shame win. Because if I leave this out, I become complicit in the silence that kept me trapped for so long.

"How could you let a pedophile around your kids?"

It was my husband who first asked the question. And he wasn't the only one.

The question wasn't just a question. It was an accusation. It carried the weight of judgment, of blame, of everything I had spent years internalising about myself.

How could I?

How could I not have seen it sooner?

How could I have let my past distort my present?

The answer is not simple. It lives in the tangled web of survival, trauma and a lifetime of conditioning.

And like most survivors, I didn't see the trap until I'd already paid the price.

The Power of Grooming and Cognitive Dissonance

Cognitive dissonance is the mental discomfort that arises when our beliefs, values, or actions are in conflict with one another. For me, it was the gap between knowing, deep down, that what had happened to me was wrong and the coping mechanisms I developed to survive.

I was groomed from the age of seven to believe that my needs didn't matter and that my primary role was to protect the abuser and the family. This grooming created a distorted reality where I prioritised keeping the peace over acknowledging my pain. The messages I internalised—about loyalty, family and silence—ran so deep that they became automatic, shaping my decisions even as an adult.

When my children were born, those same distorted beliefs lingered. I told myself that I could control the situation. The cognitive dissonance became a balancing act: I rationalised that as long as my abuser was never alone with them, they would be safe. I created rules in my mind, convincing myself that these boundaries were enough to protect them. In doing so, I avoided confronting the deeper truth: that any contact with him, no matter how supervised, was harmful to all of us.

I didn't sit down and decide to allow my abuser near my children. It wasn't a conscious, logical choice. It happened the way grooming always does—slowly, insidiously, rewiring the way I saw the world. My mind bent reality to make it survivable.

He can't hurt them if he's never alone with them.
He's old now, he's different.
If I keep him at a distance, I can still have a family.

I had been conditioned to protect him—at the expense of myself and now at the expense of my children. That's the thing about grooming. It doesn't end when childhood does.

The dissonance was unbearable at times, but denial became my shield. It allowed me to avoid the overwhelming shame and guilt of exposing my children to him. I told myself that I was preserving family ties, but the reality was that I was still trapped in the patterns of silence and avoidance that had been drilled into me since childhood. I couldn't face the thought of disrupting the fragile web of relationships within my family, even if it meant sacrificing my own peace—and risking my children's well-being.

The Shame That Thrives in Silence

Looking back now, I see how deeply the grooming and trauma affected every aspect of my life—even my ability to protect my own children. The shame was so profound that I didn't even recognise it as shame—it just felt like the truth.

The truth that I was broken.
The truth that I was unworthy.
The truth that I was a failure.

But these weren't truths. They were lies, planted deep inside me, watered by silence, grown in the dark. And the only way to kill them was to bring them into the light.

Shame thrives in silence and darkness. By bringing my story into the light, by speaking my truth, despite the victim-blaming and judgment, I'm finally breaking free from its hold.

I understand now that my worth isn't determined by other people's reactions to my disclosure. Some friends revealed themselves as true allies, while others showed they weren't equipped to handle my truth. That's okay. I'm learning to surround myself with people who can hold space for my story without judgment—my chosen family who understand the pain and recognise the immense courage it takes to break generational cycles of trauma.

Today, I parent my children with firm boundaries, having learnt the hardest way possible about the importance of protecting them. But I also parent my inner child—that seven-year-old girl who carried so much pain and confusion for so long. She deserves the same protection, the same fierce advocacy I now give my children. When I hear her whisper "Was it my fault?" I can finally answer with absolute certainty:

"No, sweetheart. Never. The shame was never yours to carry."

Breaking the Cycle

This journey out of the sexual abuse closet has been both brutal and beautiful. Each disclosure, each time I speak my truth, I reclaim a piece of myself. The family mythology of "sticking your head in the sand" no longer holds power over me.

I choose peace with myself instead—the kind that comes from living authentically, even when it's uncomfortable. The kind that comes from finally understanding that I am worthy of protection, of love, of taking up space with my whole, messy, healing truth.

For the first time, I don't need someone else's permission to exist as I am. I don't need my mother's understanding. I don't need society's validation. I don't even need justice.

Because I have something I never had before.

I have me.

And I will never abandon myself again.

PART II
THE LIGHT

24

STEPPING OUT OF THE DARK

Before I could step into the light, I had to face the darkness that had followed me for decades. The heavy, invisible weight of shame. For most of my life, I carried a secret that didn't belong to me. I built my world around it. Protected it. Protected *them*. Because speaking the truth didn't just mean naming what happened; it meant tearing down everything I thought was holding me together.

The shame wasn't just about what had been done to me —it was layered, complex, tangled up in love, loyalty and silence. They were my family. He was my dad. And she, my mum—I wanted to protect her more than I wanted to protect myself.

I had taken on a mothering role with her, trying to shield her from the truth, from the consequences, from the shame. I thought if I could carry it all quietly, I could spare her. But silence came at a cost.

When you grow up without a solid sense of self, it's easy to believe that your needs don't matter. That other people's comfort is more important than your truth. I didn't feel I was worth protecting. The shame buried my voice so deeply, I could barely hear it myself.

And there was something else too. Something I never wanted to admit.

I didn't want it to be true. I didn't want to be someone this had happened to. I didn't want to be *that* story.

It felt too ugly. Too taboo. Too hard to hold. The stigma was real. I wanted to pretend it didn't happen. I waited. I waited for him to die, thinking maybe then I'd be free. But I wasn't. Not until I claimed the truth for myself. Not until I finally understood that what happened to me was not my fault.

And the shame I'd carried for so long? It wasn't mine either.

This book is called *Not My Shame* because claiming those three words changed everything. They became a turning point. A mantra. A truth I returned to, again and again. It wasn't mine. It was never mine. And I don't have to carry it anymore.

Journal Prompt

What would it feel like to see your healing not as something to finish, but as something to tend to like a garden, not a race?

This chapter isn't a prescription; it's an offering. If you're on your own healing journey, you may find yourself drawn to one approach or a combination of many. My hope is that by sharing my story, you feel a little less alone and a little more empowered to begin—or continue—your own path to healing.

I'm not an expert or a therapist. I am someone who has navigated this difficult journey from the inside. I hope you will see yourself in parts of what I share, but more importantly, I hope you feel free to follow what feels right for you. Your healing doesn't have to look like mine. It doesn't have to look like anyone else's. It just has to belong to you.

Before I share the different therapies that supported my healing, I want to be clear about something important. If you're early on in your journey, this next section might feel like a lot. You might start to wonder if healing means you have to do *all* of these things—EMDR, CBT, dance therapy, tapping, IFS and more. I understand that feeling because I've been there too, staring at other people's healing paths and thinking, *Do I have to do all of that to be okay?*

The truth is, there is no single roadmap for healing. There is no magic formula, no perfect combination of modalities. What worked for me may not be what works for you. Healing is deeply personal, shaped by your history, your needs, your timing and your nervous system. Some people find deep transformation in one modality. Others move through several as they grow, change and uncover new layers.

The therapies I describe in the following pages are not a checklist. They're simply windows into what helped me at different stages of my journey. Take what resonates. Leave what doesn't. Trust your pace. The most powerful thing you can do is listen to yourself—and honour what you need, when you need it.

Healing isn't about doing it all. It's about doing what matters, in a way that's true for *you*.

Traditional Talking Therapy: The Power of Being Heard

Sometimes, the most powerful healing comes from simply being heard and understood. Traditional talking therapy gave me that for the first time.

I still remember the first time I sat in a therapist's office, my hands gripping the edges of the chair. I had no idea what to say. Where do you even begin when your past feels like a shattered mirror?

Talking therapy was my first experience of structured healing. For so long, my truth had lived in the shadows, hidden behind silence and survival. But in that room, with a therapist who listened not out of obligation, but out of genuine care, my words finally had a place to exist.

She didn't recoil. She didn't question whether I was telling the truth. She simply listened. And in doing so, she gave me something I had never had before: validation. The kind that says, *I believe you and you deserved better.*

Not every therapist was the right fit. Some sessions felt repetitive, like I was circling the same pain with no way out. There were moments I left feeling lighter and others where I questioned whether therapy was even helping. But even in the frustrating moments, I was unraveling something. Pulling at threads that had been knotted for decades.

It wasn't a quick fix, but it was a start.

Journal Prompt

What truth of yours is still waiting to be heard and who might be safe enough to hear it?

EMDR (Eye Movement Desensitisation and Reprocessing)

EMDR is a trauma-focused therapy that helps people process and heal from distressing memories. It involves recalling traumatic events while engaging in specific bilateral stimulation, such as guided eye movements, tapping, or sounds. This process helps the brain rewire how the memories are stored, so they lose their emotional intensity and no longer feel overwhelming.

I had been undergoing EMDR therapy for a year. I was finally ready to face my trauma head-on and begin processing the most painful memories. It was some of the hardest emotional work I've ever done, but also some of the most transformative. In the Appendix, I included an interview with Lucy, my EMDR therapist. She, too, is a survivor of sexual abuse and brings a unique blend of professional skill and lived experience. Her insights into trauma, healing and resilience are powerful. I hope her words offer you the same clarity and comfort they've given me.

Cognitive Behavioural Therapy (CBT): Rewiring the Inner Voice

CBT is a structured and evidence-based approach that helps people identify and challenge unhelpful thoughts and beliefs. The idea behind CBT is that our thoughts, feelings and behaviours are connected. By changing how we think, we can shift how we feel and act. It is especially effective for anxiety, depression and trauma recovery, offering practical tools to reframe negative thinking patterns and build healthier mental habits.

In therapy, I learned how to spot my automatic thoughts, the stories my mind told me without question and then examine them for accuracy. My therapist often used thought records, where I'd write down a triggering situation, the thought that followed, how it made me feel and what a more balanced response might be. We explored core beliefs I had held for decades, often without realising it and traced them back to their roots.

CBT helped me realise something I wish I had known sooner: thoughts are not facts. For years, my mind had been wired for survival. Fear, shame and self-blame weren't just emotions. They were my internal soundtrack. CBT helped me challenge that.

I had spent so long believing: *I am unlovable. I am a burden. I am broken.* But where had those beliefs come from? Were they mine? Or had they been given to me by those who hurt me?

One of the most pivotal moments in therapy came when I was taught to challenge my automatic thoughts. If someone was late to meet me, my mind jumped to: I'm not important. They don't care about me. But my therapist gently asked, "Is that a fact, or is that a feeling?"

That one question shifted everything. CBT gave me tools to untangle myself from the mental loops that had kept me stuck. Slowly, thought by thought, I began to rewrite the narrative I had lived inside for so long.

Journal Prompt

Is there a thought you've believed for years that might actually be a feeling—or a story you're ready to rewrite?

Somatic Healing: When the Body Speaks

I had spent decades trying to ignore my body; I wanted to numb and escape it. But somatic healing asked me to *listen* to it instead. I came to learn something I had never been taught: trauma doesn't just live in your memories. It lives in your muscles, your breath and your nervous system. Talking helped me name my story. But somatic work helped me release it.

EFT: Tapping and Truth-Telling

EFT (Emotional Freedom Techniques), often called "tapping," is a mind-body practice that combines elements of cognitive therapy with acupressure. By tapping on specific meridian points on the face and body while speaking out loud about painful thoughts or feelings, EFT helps release emotional blocks and calm the nervous system. The underlying philosophy is that unresolved emotional distress disrupts the body's energy system. By addressing both the emotion and the body at the same time, healing becomes possible.

It felt silly at first, tapping my face and saying, "Even though I feel broken, I deeply and completely love and accept myself." But over time, something in me shifted. Gently. Quietly. EFT gave me a way to access the feelings I didn't have words for yet and offered me permission to let them move through.

Movement and Dance: Truth in Motion

As a child, movement was freedom. I would run through the park, climb trees, feel the wind in my hair and the ground solid beneath me.

As a young adult, it became something else. I danced in clubs, high or drunk, disconnected from my body. The music drowned out the pain and the movement became a form of dissociation.

But here in dance therapy, it was different. This time, I was sober, present and willing to feel. There was no choreography. Just truth in motion, a sacred and wordless language that allowed me to process emotions I couldn't yet speak aloud.

Breath-work: Coming Home to My Body

Breath work became a bridge between chaos and calm. Slow, intentional breath told my nervous system: *you are safe now*. Some sessions felt like emotional exorcisms. Others were quiet, grounding, anchoring. But every single time, the breath brought me back.

Journal Prompt

> What would it feel like to ask your body—not your mind—what it needs today?

Acceptance and Commitment Therapy (ACT): Walking With, Not Away

ACT asked me to stop trying to fix everything and to start being with myself instead. I had always believed healing meant becoming pain-free. ACT gently corrected that belief. Pain and healing can walk side by side.

It taught me to notice my thoughts without becoming them. To say, "Ah, there's that story again," and keep moving forward anyway. It asked me to connect with my values and to live from that place—even if fear, shame or grief were still in the room. Especially then.

ACT reminded me: I didn't have to wait until I was healed to begin again.

Journal Prompt

> What would your life look like if healing didn't mean waiting to feel "ready," but instead meant acting from love —even in the presence of fear?

Closing Anchor: From Surviving to Belonging

None of these therapies gave me a finish line. But they gave me tools. They gave me language. They gave me a choice. Most of all, they gave me back to myself.

Other Healing Modalities to Explore

The therapies I've shared in this book are the ones that shaped my healing journey. But they're not the only options. Just as every trauma experience is unique, so too is the path to recovery. While I can only speak directly to the approaches I've personally used, I want to acknowledge a few other therapeutic modalities that many trauma survivors have found helpful.

Dialectical Behaviour Therapy (DBT)

DBT was originally developed for individuals with Borderline Personality Disorder (BPD), but it has since become a powerful tool for those navigating Complex PTSD, emotional dysregulation and self-destructive coping mechanisms. DBT combines elements of mindfulness, distress tolerance, emotional regulation and interpersonal effectiveness. For survivors who find it difficult to directly confront traumatic memories in CBT or EMDR, DBT can offer a stabilising foundation and help build the skills needed to feel safe in the body before deeper trauma work begins.

Art Therapy

Art therapy offers a non-verbal route to healing. For many survivors, putting pain into words can feel impossible at first. Art, whether through drawing, painting, collage, or sculpture, can bypass the rational mind and give voice to emotions stored in the body. It's not about artistic skill. It's about expression, release and sometimes discovering what you didn't know was waiting to be seen.

Group Therapy and Peer Support

Group therapy, survivor circles and peer-led spaces can be profoundly validating. They remind us we are not alone and help dismantle the shame that often keeps trauma hidden.

This chapter of the book was about tending to the mind and body, but I hadn't yet looked deeper. Beneath the wounds were younger parts of me still stuck in the past, still longing to be seen. That's where we go next. Because healing doesn't just ask what happened to you. It asks, what have you carried for too long? And, are you ready to lay it down?

25

MY INTERNAL FAMILY (IFS)

Simon had become a good friend and in many ways, a quiet guide. He often talked about Internal Family Systems (IFS). "Love all your parts," he'd say. I must admit, I'd roll my eyes. *No more woo-woo spiritual stuff, please.*

Still, his enthusiasm was infectious. He never preached or pushed. He simply pointed me back to myself. His calm presence and unwavering belief in healing created space for me to begin believing too. Looking back, I can see how pivotal his presence was in my life. He didn't rescue me. He walked beside me, holding the light steady until I was ready to find my own.

"Wow, I have another day. To live, to breathe, to experience this wonderful life. Everything is perfect." That was Simon.

When he said "love all your parts," something in me softened. I decided to follow this trailhead. Maybe this wasn't just more spiritual fluff. Maybe it was something deeper.

IFS Insight

In IFS therapy, a trailhead is an entry point, something that draws our attention inward. It could be a persistent emotion, an old belief, or a physical sensation. A part of us asking to be seen.

Simon recommended a book: *No Bad Parts* by Richard C. Schwartz, Ph.D. In it, Schwartz explains that we're not one fixed self, but a system of parts, each with its own role, needs and voice. Even parts we dislike, like anxiety or people-pleasing, are trying to protect us, often using strategies learned in childhood.

At the centre of this system is the "Self": calm, compassionate and capable of leading with clarity. This idea shifted something in me. I wasn't broken. I was just complex. And maybe all those parts I'd hidden weren't wrong. They were trying to help.

In IFS, the parts that hold our deepest wounds are called exiles. These are often younger versions of ourselves, our inner children, who carry pain we weren't able to process at the time. They're hidden away to protect us, but they never stop longing to be seen, heard and healed.

While IFS is a comprehensive therapeutic model developed by Dr Richard C. Schwartz, I'm not an IFS expert, I'm simply someone sharing my personal experience of how this therapy helped me connect with parts of myself I had long ignored. If this resonates with you, there are many trained professionals, books and resources available to support you in exploring it more deeply.

I began to understand that I'd been carrying unprocessed

trauma for years. I had built walls, worn masks and locked parts of myself away to survive. IFS gave me a map to explore those inner landscapes. It was fascinating and terrifying.

Connecting with my parts, especially my inner child, felt overwhelming. How could I face the emotions of a child who had endured so much? But I knew real healing would take courage. The courage to sit with the most wounded part of me and offer her the compassion she'd always deserved.

Meeting My Inner Child

One of my exiles—the part of me I came to know as my inner child—had been locked away for years. I could feel her tug, a quiet ache I could no longer ignore. So I sat down, closed my eyes and imagined meeting her.

Me: Hi there...

Little Daniela: Hi. Who are you?

Me: I'm you... I'm the grown-up version of you. I've been wanting to meet you for so long.

Little Daniela: Why are you here now?

Me: Because I'm sorry I've been away. You've been so brave and I know how hard it's been.

Little Daniela: It's been really hard. I didn't know what to do.

Me: I know, sweet girl. You went through things no child should ever have to. You didn't know it wasn't supposed to be like that, did you?

Little Daniela: No. I thought it was my fault. My brothers didn't have to do what I did. It seemed really unfair.

Me: It was never your fault. You were just a child. None of it was your responsibility.

Little Daniela: But I felt like it was...

Me: I wish I could've been there to tell you that you didn't have to carry that. But you survived. You found safety in school, in sports, in the things you loved. That was clever of you.

Little Daniela: I just wanted to feel okay.

Me: And you did everything you could. I'm so proud of you. I'm here now. Can I sit with you?

Little Daniela: Okay...

Me: You don't have to talk. I just want to be with you. You never got to feel safe enough to share how you really felt.

Little Daniela: I wasn't allowed to cry. Or be angry. I had to keep it all inside.

Me: That wasn't fair. Your feelings matter. You deserve to feel, to be held. I'm here to listen.

Little Daniela: Really?

Me: *Really*. I'll always listen. And when you're ready, we can go play.

Little Daniela: Play?

Me: Yes. See the butterflies? We'll run until we're out of breath, then lie in the grass and laugh until our bellies hurt.

Little Daniela: That sounds fun...

Me: It will be. And I'll remind you again: It was not your fault. You deserved love, safety, encouragement.

Little Daniela: But I didn't get that...

Me: No. And I'm so sorry. I can't change the past, but I'm here now. You're part of me and I promise I'll never leave you again.

Little Daniela: Really?

Me: *Really*. There's a space in my heart just for you. *Always*.

Little Daniela: Will everything be okay?

Me: Yes, my brave girl. You're going to heal. You'll break the cycle. You'll build the life you deserve. You'll become the kind of mum you always needed. And it will be beautiful.

Little Daniela: Do I really matter?

Me: You matter so much. I love you. *Always*.

Little Daniela: I think I'm ready to play now.

Me: Let's go.

∽

Letters to My Inner Child

Alongside dialogue, I began writing letters. This became another powerful way to connect.

∽

Dear Precious Inner Child,

I'm so sorry it took me this long to reach you. But I'm here now and I promise not to ignore you again. You didn't deserve what happened. It wasn't your fault. The adults failed you. But I won't.

You carried burdens no child should. You stayed silent. You became the peacekeeper. But none of that was yours to hold.

Now we're free. Free to speak, to feel, to laugh and cry. You get to be seen, loved, celebrated. I'll protect you fiercely. Every day, I'll remind you: You are safe. You are loved. You matter.

Would you like to come out and play?

With all my love,

Your Adult Self

∼

Dear Grown-Up Me,

OMG—we're actually free?! This is AMAZING! It feels like I've been stuck in a dark cage forever. But now I can run, jump and be me again!

Can we go roller skating? Go swimming? Stay up late eating popcorn? I just want to be seen and laugh more. No more bullies, okay?

We're superheroes. We made it.

Love and a million hugs,

Little You

∼

Journal Prompts: *The Power of Parts Work*

- What parts of you are hardest to love? Could they be trying to protect you in their own way?
- What did you love doing as a child? What's stopping you from doing it now?

- If you could go back and say one thing to your inner child, what would it be?

Healing Exercises:

Your inner child still lives within you—holding memories, unmet needs, and quiet longings for love, safety and joy. These simple practices are an invitation to reconnect with that part of you. Whether through words, imagination or play, each one is a step toward healing, integration and compassion.

Write to Your Inner Child

Start with: "Dear Inner Child, I want you to know..."
   Or: "If I could go back and be there for you, I would..."

Guided Visualisation

Close your eyes. Picture a safe space. Invite your inner child to sit beside you. Notice what they want to say.

Reclaim Joy

Choose one thing you loved as a child and do it this week. Let joy lead the way.

Final Reflection

Healing doesn't mean forgetting. It means remembering with compassion. It means choosing, again and again, to love all your parts, even the ones that once felt unlovable.

As I sat with these parts, I began to see they weren't random behaviours. They were survival strategies, formed long before I had words. I started to trace the threads backward, to the ache for connection, the fear of abandonment and the need to disappear.

That path led me home.

Home to my attachment wounds.

26

THE ATTACHMENTS THAT SHAPE US

When I first heard the term *attachment wounds*, it felt like a clinical label for something far more visceral: the invisible scars etched into my nervous system. A map of survival drawn by Little Daniela.

I was seven years old when my world shattered. *Seven.* An age when most children are learning to ride bicycles, memorising simple multiplication, believing in the absolute safety of their parents' cuddles. Those early years of abuse didn't just steal my childhood. They rewired my understanding of connection, of intimacy, of belonging. Every touch became a potential threat.

I learnt to fragment myself—to become small, to disappear. Survival's most intricate magic trick.

I've come to understand this rewiring through the lens of attachment theory, a psychological framework that explores how our earliest bonds, crucial for survival and developing a fundamental sense of self, shape our relationships throughout life. The works of John Bowlby and Mary Ainsworth and more recently the book *Attached* by Dr. Amir Levine and Rachel Heller, helped me see the patterns I'd been caught in for years.

What I hadn't realised, as an adult, was that so much of what I needed was already within me. What I had been seeking externally, sometimes desperately, was validation.

I would get deeply attached to friendships, hoping that maybe this one would finally understand me. Maybe this friend would save me. But friendships, I've learned, are about mutual support, not about one person filling the emotional holes of the other. That expectation placed an unfair burden on those relationships and left me feeling crushed when people inevitably couldn't meet those unconscious needs.

As I worked with these patterns, I began to recognise that the hurt I was carrying wasn't coming from just one place. It was coming from multiple parts of me. There was the inner child, still aching to be chosen and soothed. There was the inner protector, constantly scanning for danger or rejection. And slowly, another voice began to emerge too: my inner best friend. The one who could say, "Hey, you're okay. You're not too much. You're learning."

Over time, I came to understand these voices as different aspects of my internal world:

- **The inner child** – tender, wounded, longing for reassurance and safety
- **The inner parent** – grounded, wise, capable of protecting and guiding
- **The inner best friend** – gentle, encouraging and full of compassion

Learning to hear these voices and eventually speak to myself from a place of care, wasn't just healing; it was rebalancing. I was no longer seeking a saviour in someone else. I was learning to be what I needed, from the inside out.

And then I began to notice the patterns.

Why hasn't she texted me back? Did I do something wrong? Are they ghosting me?

Then, a gentler voice began to interrupt:

"Daniela, you may be the main character in your story, but everyone else is the main character in theirs. Life is busy. There are often things going on that you won't be aware of."

And then: "Don't be so needy."

That part still makes me smile. Life really is a balance, isn't it? That phrase, "Don't be so needy," became a doorway to a deeper truth. I wasn't too much. I just had unmet needs. And part of healing meant learning how to assert those needs with kindness, rather than suppress them or hand them over to someone else to fix.

As I grew into my awareness, my friendships became more balanced. I was no longer the rescuer. No longer the invisible one. No longer the victim. I was becoming someone who could connect without losing herself.

Journal Prompt: *Understanding Your Attachment Style*

Which attachment style feels most familiar to you? There's no "good" or "bad" style, just adaptive strategies we developed to survive early relational dynamics. As we grow in awareness, we can move toward more secure ways of connecting.

Secure Attachment

Description: You're generally comfortable with both intimacy and independence. You have a balanced view of relationships, communicate your needs effectively and honestly without shame, navigate conflict constructively and allow space for closeness and autonomy.

Origins: This attachment style typically develops from a history of consistent, responsive and attuned caregiving. Caregivers were reliably available, sensitive to your needs and provided comfort and support.

Inner Monologue: "I am worthy of love and support. Others are generally trustworthy and available. I can handle challenges in relationships."

Anxious Attachment

Description: You crave closeness but often fear rejection and abandonment. You may overthink, over-function, or seek frequent reassurance. Others may have described you as "clingy" or "overly dependent".

Origins: The anxious attachment style often arises from inconsistent or unpredictable caregiving. Your caregiver might have been loving and attentive at times but neglectful or unavailable at other times, creating a sense of uncertainty and insecurity in your formative years.

Inner Monologue: "I need to be close to others to feel safe, but I worry they will leave me. I often feel insecure and unworthy of love. My needs are not always met."

Avoidant Attachment

Description: You value independence and self-reliance. You may experience discomfort around emotional closeness and downplay the importance of relationships. As you are inherently uncomfortable with intimacy or showing vulnerability, you may find it difficult to establish deep interpersonal relationships with shared emotional expression.

Origins: The avoidant attachment type typically develops from an emotionally unavailable or rejecting caregiver. They may have been dismissive of your needs, discouraged your emotional expression, or emphasised independence at the expense of interpersonal connection.

Inner Monologue: "I am strong and self-sufficient. I don't need others to rely on. Emotional closeness is uncomfortable and can lead to disappointment. I prefer to keep my distance."

Disorganised Attachment (Fearful-Avoidant)

Description: A little bit anxious, a little bit avoidant, you both desire and fear intimacy. Your relationships may feel chaotic, unpredictable and confusing. As a result, you may have difficulty trusting others.

Origins: Those with a disorganised attachment type are often survivors of abuse, neglect, trauma, or inconsistent caregiving, where the caregiver was a source of both comfort and fear. In turn, your inner child has come to associate relationships with both safety and danger.

Inner Monologue: "I want to be loved, but love is dangerous. I don't know who to trust or how to feel safe in relationships. I feel confused and overwhelmed by my need for connection and my fear of it."

Journal Prompts: *Gentle Questions for Self-Reflection*

- What patterns do you notice in your closest relationships?
- How do you respond to distance, conflict, or unmet needs?
- What would it feel like to offer your younger self the steady love and reassurance they needed?
- What does safety in connection look like for you now?

Connecting with my inner child and the many parts of me that had once felt exiled, served as a turning point. I no longer saw myself as broken, but as beautifully complex. Every coping mechanism, every reaction, had once served a purpose: survival.

But as I listened more deeply to those parts, a bigger question began to surface: *Where did all this pain begin?*

The anxiety, the people-pleasing, the constant vigilance—they weren't just personality quirks. They were rooted in something older. Something deeper. Trauma.

To move forward, I had to understand what trauma really was. Not just in theory, but in the body, in the nervous system, in the shape of my life. And what I found was that even in the wreckage, growth was possible.

27

UNDERSTANDING TRAUMA AND POST-TRAUMATIC GROWTH

For years, I thought trauma meant I was broken. That if I couldn't just "get over it," there was something deeply wrong with me. I looked at the world around me: people laughing, working, living. I wondered how they did it. How did they move so freely while I felt stuck behind an invisible wall?

Back then, I didn't realise that trauma doesn't always look like flashbacks or nightmares. Sometimes it looks like overworking. Or people pleasing. Or never letting yourself be still. Sometimes it whispers:

You're too much.
You don't belong here.
You are just a loser.

What is Complex PTSD?

Complex Post-Traumatic Stress Disorder (C-PTSD) takes the symptoms of PTSD and sprinkles on extras: emotional dysregulation, distorted or negative sense of self and quite often, difficulties in forming and maintaining healthy, stable relationships. C-PTSD isn't caused by one single traumatic event. It's what happens when pain forms a pattern of chronic and prolonged trauma. When traumas happen in a repetitive loop, especially in childhood, the feeling of being trapped or having no escape occupies the core self-construct. It's like building your life on sand. Everything may look fine from the outside, but reality presents an unstable and insecure foundation, feeling as though you could be knocked down at any given moment. For me, C-PTSD showed up as:

- Feeling like I was fundamentally different from everyone else
- Struggling to manage my emotions or trust my instincts
- Being hyper-independent, yet deeply afraid of abandonment
- A continuous loop of shame, self-blame and emotional exhaustion

It was a lonely, confusing place to live. But here's what no one tells you in those early days of healing: there's another side to this story.

The Possibility of Growth

Post-Traumatic Growth (PTG) doesn't mean being grateful for what happened. It means discovering that healing can lead to something unexpectedly beautiful. Not because trauma was a gift—because it isn't. It is because you chose to grow anyway. You *chose* to turn your wounds into wisdom.

Beware of Toxic Positivity

Truth matters. Even when it's messy. *Especially* when it's messy.

As I moved deeper into my healing journey, I noticed a quiet pressure, internally and externally, to always look on the bright side, to stay strong, to be grateful. And while gratitude has been a powerful part of my recovery, there's a difference between gratitude and denial.

I began to recognise something that didn't sit quite right. Phrases like:

- "Everything happens for a reason."
- "At least it wasn't worse."
- "Just stay positive!"
- "Good vibes only."

On the surface, they sound hopeful. But when you're in pain, they can feel like a dismissal; like someone's handing you a smiley face sticker to cover a deep wound.

This is toxic positivity–when the pressure to appear

happy or "fine" overrides the permission to be real. It's a false kind of light, one that blinds instead of illuminates.

Toxic positivity says:

- "Don't feel that."
- "Don't talk about that."
- "Keep it upbeat."

Healing says:

- "It's okay to feel this."
- "Let's talk about it."
- "You're safe here, even in your mess."

We don't heal by pretending we're not hurting. We heal by telling the truth about our pain and allowing the light in after we've honoured the dark.

Holding Both the Dark and the Light

Healing invites us to hold complexity. You can feel joy and grief. Hope and heartbreak. Growth and discomfort. Instead of reaching for artificial sunshine, I began saying things like:

- "This is hard and I'm doing my best."
- "I can feel sadness and still be okay."
- "I don't have to be positive; I just have to be present."

Journal Prompt: *What Do You Really Need?*

> When you're hurting, what feels more comforting? A voice that tells you to cheer up? Or one that simply sits beside you and says, "I'm here. Take your time."

Write a list of genuinely supportive phrases you can offer yourself or others when things are hard.
Some to get you started:

- "It makes sense you feel this way."
- "You don't have to fix this right now."
- "I see how heavy this is. You're not alone."

Final Thoughts

Real healing doesn't demand a smile. It welcomes truth. It meets you where you are. And it reminds you:
You don't have to fake the light to be worthy of love.
You are enough, even in the shadows. *Especially* in the shadows.

Post-traumatic Growth

Richard Tedeschi, Ph.D., and Lawrence Calhoun, Ph.D., psychologists from the University of North Carolina, developed the Post-Traumatic Growth Inventory (PTGI)—a 21-item scale based on a five-factor model. Each pillar reflects a domain where positive psychological change can occur after trauma. Here's what that looks like for me:

Relating to Others

I used to hide parts of myself to be accepted. Since then, healing has taught me that real connection comes from being seen. As I began to share my truth, I attracted people who could meet me there, with empathy, not pity.

New Possibilities

I never imagined I'd write a book. Or become a yoga teacher. Or hold space for others in their healing. But when trauma cracked my world open, it made room for something new to grow.

Personal Strength

I used to believe I was weak for breaking down. Now I see the strength it took to keep going, to speak my truth and to rebuild my life. Surviving isn't weakness; it is resilience in its rawest form.

Spiritual Change

My faith was once rooted in fear and shame. Rebuilding it was messy, but necessary. I now find spirituality in stillness, in nature, in breath and in the quiet knowing that I am part of something bigger than my pain.

Appreciation of Life

I started noticing things I'd never paid much mind to before: the warmth of the sun on my skin, the sound of my child's laughter, the calm after a storm. Joy became more vibrant because I knew what it was to live without it.

28

UNDERSTANDING THE NERVOUS SYSTEM – WHY TRAUMA LIVES IN THE BODY

For a long time, I believed healing was something that happened in the mind. If I could just think differently—if I could fix my thoughts—then maybe the anxiety, the sadness and the exhaustion would lift.

But trauma doesn't just live in the mind. It takes root in the body. If you've ever had a wave of anxiety hit out of nowhere, or shut down in moments of emotional intensity, or felt numb when you should feel joy, this isn't 'just in your head', it's your nervous system speaking. Reacting. Trying to protect you.

Why the Nervous System Matters

Your nervous system is your body's built-in safety system. It was designed to protect you, automatically and instantly. When a threat (real or perceived) shows up, your body responds before your brain even has a chance to think.

Your autonomic nervous system has two main branches:

Sympathetic Nervous System (SNS)

This is your fight-or-flight mode. It mobilises energy to prepare your body for action in response to perceived danger or distress. Your heart races, your pupils dilate for enhanced vision, your muscles tense for quick movement, your breathing rate increases in an effort to supply more oxygen and you release stress hormones like adrenaline and cortisol. SNS exists as a crucial matter of survival, enabling you to confront a threat or escape from it.

Parasympathetic Nervous System (PNS)

And here we have your rest-and-digest mode. This serves to conserve energy and promote relaxation, calming the body after a stressful episode, helping you to recover, connect and feel safe. Here, you'll notice your breathing has slowed down, your muscles become more relaxed and your heart rate slows down. The purpose of the PNS is to facilitate healing, growth and social connection.

In a healthy system, we move fluidly between these two states. But trauma, especially chronic or developmental trauma, can throw this balance off. We often get stuck in survival mode, long after the danger has passed.

Polyvagal Theory: A New Lens on Safety

Dr. Stephen Porges' Polyvagal Theory offers a deeper understanding of how our nervous system helps us respond to cues of safety and threat in our environment. Based on this assessment, we respond in predictable ways, which Porges has described as a *hierarchy of responses*. A key component of this system is the vagus nerve, the superhighway connecting the brain, body and heart. It helps us to regulate our emotions, connect with others and feel safe.

When our nervous system perceives a threat, it may activate one of the following responses:

- **Fight:** Anger, irritability, control, defensiveness
- **Flight:** Anxiety, restlessness, perfectionism, overworking, avoidance
- **Freeze:** Numbness, disconnection, shutdown, dissociation, immobility
- **Fawn:** People-pleasing, lack of boundaries, over-accommodation, excessive compliance

These responses are not flaws; they are adaptive strategies the body develops to enhance the probability of survival. The empowering truth is that our nervous system has the capacity to adapt and learn new patterns. With support, it can learn to recognise and respond to safety in the present.

Five Tools to Regulate the Nervous System

Healing isn't just about understanding your trauma—it's also about actively cultivating a sense of safety. These small, body-based practices can help bring your system back into balance.

1. Breath Work – Reset Through the Breath

Our breath is one of the most immediate tools we have to regulate the nervous system.

- *Longer exhales:* Inhale for 4, exhale for 6–8. This slows the heart rate.
- *Box breathing:* Inhale 4 → hold 4 → exhale 4 → hold 4.
- *Sighing or humming:* Activates the vagus nerve through sound and vibration. Try humming quietly or letting out a soft, audible "aaah."

2. Cold Exposure – A Gentle Jolt of Presence

Brief cold exposure can stimulate the vagus nerve and promote alertness, followed by a return to calm.

- Splash cold water on your face
- Finish a shower with 30 seconds of cold water
- Hold an ice cube in your hand (with caution)
- Take a cold plunge if appropriate for your health and comfort level

3. Grounding – Come Back Into Your Body

Grounding techniques anchor you in the present, especially when feeling dissociated or overwhelmed.

- *5-4-3-2-1 senses:* Name 5 things you see, 4 you feel, 3 you hear, 2 you smell, 1 you taste
- *Walk barefoot:* Let the earth remind you that you belong here
- *Touch:* Hold a smooth stone, soft fabric, or warm mug. Engage your tactile senses.

4. Movement – Let Your Body Speak

Trauma that has no place to go, stays stuck. Movement can help release pent-up energy and emotions.

- Gently shake out your limbs to release tension
- Stretch slowly or try gentle yoga
- Dance freely—allow your body to move freely and intuitively

5. Sound and Vibration – Calm Through Resonance

Sound and vibration influence our nervous system and reconnect us to rhythm and safety.

- Hum, sing, or chant to stimulate the vagus nerve through vibration
- Listen to calming music with slow rhythms
- Repeat a soothing mantra such as: *"I am safe"*

Final Thoughts: Your Body Is On Your Side

I used to think that something was wrong with me. That I was weak. Too sensitive. Broken. But learning about the nervous system changed everything. I realised my body wasn't the problem. It was my protector. It had just never been told the danger had passed.

If you recognise yourself in the freeze... in the fawn... in the flood of anxiety—please hear this:

You are *not* broken.

You are *not* dramatic or "too much."

You *are* a survivor of circumstances that asked your body to carry too much, too soon, for too long.

And healing *is* possible.

The goal isn't to avoid stress forever—but to help your body remember: I'm safe now.

Bit by bit. Breath by breath.

You can come home to yourself.

You deserve to feel calm.

You deserve to feel safe.

You deserve to belong to your body again.

Journal Prompt

> What are three things that help your body feel safe, soothed, or settled? Choose one and practice it this week—not as a performance, but as an act of love.

As I began to regulate my nervous system and feel safer in my own body, I started to get curious about the deeper chemistry behind my moods, energy and emotional shifts. Why did some days feel heavy and flat, while others felt bright and full of hope, even when nothing had changed externally?

I wanted to understand not just my thoughts and responses, but the inner workings of my brain. What I discovered about neurotransmitters, those tiny messengers of the mind, gave me language, clarity and a deeper compassion for myself.

Because sometimes what feels like a flaw is simply chemistry looking for balance.

29

UNDERSTANDING YOUR DAILY D.O.S.E

Our brains are like personal pharmacies, constantly producing chemicals that influence our emotions, energy and overall well-being. Understanding how these neurochemicals work can empower us to intentionally activate them, naturally enhancing our happiness, resilience and motivation.

One day, while talking to Simon, he pointed out something I'll never forget: four key neurochemicals associated with positivity spell out a handy mnemonic device: D.O.S.E. —Dopamine, Oxytocin, Serotonin and Endorphins.

Each of these neurochemicals plays a unique role in how we experience joy, connection, motivation and peace. And the best part? We can support their release through small, daily actions.

Let's break down what each one does, why it matters and how we can support our bodies in creating this inner chemistry of well-being.

Dopamine: The Motivation and Reward Neurotransmitter

Dopamine is the neurotransmitter responsible for motivation, focus and that satisfying feeling of accomplishment. It's released when we set goals, take action and achieve something. Even small wins can trigger dopamine release.

When does it release naturally?

Anytime we experience reward or progress; completing a task, learning something new, or receiving positive feedback.

Why does it matter?

Low dopamine levels can contribute to procrastination, low energy and difficulty experiencing pleasure (anhedonia). By supporting healthy dopamine function, we can enhance drive, energy and a sense of accomplishment.

Ways to boost dopamine:

- Set and complete small, achievable goals
- Create a daily to-do list and tick off completed items
- Celebrate successes, both big and small
- Listen to upbeat, energising music
- Seek out new and novel experiences

- Organise and declutter a small area (yes, even your junk drawer)
- Engage in creative expression (e.g. writing, painting, music)
- Play mentally engaging games or learn a new skill
- Visualise a future success that you're working toward

Oxytocin: The Bonding & Connection Hormone

Oxytocin is often called the "love hormone". This neurochemical is released during positive social interactions and physical closeness, helping us feel safe and connected to others.

When does it release naturally?

Oxytocin release is stimulated by physical touch (like hugs), acts of kindness, social intimacy, sustained eye contact and heartfelt connection.

Why does it matter?

We're wired for connection. Oxytocin helps to counter the effects of stress hormones and promotes empathy, which strengthens social bonds and contributes to our sense of belonging.

Ways to boost oxytocin:

- Hug someone for 20 seconds or longer
- Spend focused, quality time with loved ones
- Express gratitude or offer a sincere compliment
- Engage in acts of kindness or volunteer
- Cuddle with a pet
- Write a heartfelt message to someone you care about
- Watch a touching film or read an uplifting story
- Hold hands, make eye contact, or share a laugh
- Join a supportive community or group

Serotonin: The Mood Stabiliser

Serotonin is a neurotransmitter that plays a crucial role in mood regulation, promoting feelings of calm, stability and well-being. It also helps regulate appetite, sleep and digestion.

When does it release naturally?

Serotonin release is associated with feelings of safety, accomplishment and social connection. Practices like mindfulness, gratitude and gentle movement can also support serotonin levels.

Why does it matter?

Imbalances in serotonin levels are associated with mood disorders such as depression and anxiety. Supporting healthy serotonin function helps to stabilise mood and promote emotional resilience.

Ways to boost serotonin:

- Spend at least 10 minutes daily in sunlight (but don't forget the sunblock!)
- Practice mindfulness meditation or deep breathing exercises
- Consume foods rich in tryptophan (e.g. bananas, nuts, eggs)
- Reflect on a happy memory
- Journal your gratitude
- Walk in nature, slowly and mindfully
- Listen to calming music
- Drink water—hydration supports brain health
- Practise self-compassion and positive self-talk
- Reconnect with small joys from your past

Endorphins: The Body's Natural Pain Relievers and Mood Boosters

Endorphins are your body's natural feel-good chemicals. These neurochemicals act as natural analgesics, reducing pain and promoting feelings of pleasure and euphoria. They are released in response to physical activity and other stimulating experiences.

When does it release naturally?

Endorphin release is triggered by physical exercise, laughter, music and other pleasurable and exciting experiences.

Why does it matter?

Endorphins help us bounce back from stress, alleviate pain, enhance our mood and contribute to a sense of vitality and well-being.

Ways to boost endorphins:

- Engage in regular exercise—even 20 minutes makes a difference
- Laugh! Watch a comedy or be silly with a friend
- Dance like nobody's watching
- Sing in the shower or belt it out in the car
- Consume spicy foods (yes, really—capsaicin can trigger endorphin release)
- Try something adventurous
- Take a cold shower or splash cold water on your face
- Cuddle with a pet or play with a child
- Do something that makes you feel strong and empowered

Your Daily D.O.S.E. Reflection

Every day is different. Some days you might be bursting with energy. Others, you might just be trying to get through. Let your D.O.S.E. practice meet you where you are.
  Try this:

- Choose one small action from any category today
- If you feel up to it, try one from each—for a full "daily dose"
- Mix and match based on what you need: Connection? Calm? Motivation?
- Reflect at the end of the day: What worked? What did you enjoy?

Final Thoughts

Happiness isn't about getting it right every day. It's about gentle, consistent practices that remind your mind and body how to feel good. By understanding your brain's built-in chemistry and choosing small habits that can help to activate it, you become the chemist of your own well-being. You don't need to chase external fixes. So much of what you need is already within you.

  Learning about my brain's natural D.O.S.E. gave me a powerful tool: a way to understand myself. A lens for my moods. A rhythm to my motivation. It helped me see why some days felt like swimming through sunlight and others like sinking in fog.

  But even as I began to nurture these feel-good neurochemicals through daily habits, I sensed something deeper calling. Because understanding science was one thing, but learning how to truly love myself? That was another journey entirely.

I could boost dopamine with a to-do list, soak in oxytocin from a hug and dance my way into endorphins... but if I didn't also meet myself with compassion, especially on those hard days, it would never feel like enough. It wasn't about chasing a chemical shift; it was about creating a connection that felt steady, kind and real.

So I turned inward again. Not to fix myself, but to *befriend* myself. To become the one who stays, especially when things feel messy or hard.

When the Books Aren't Enough

A gentle nudge for my fellow self-help junkies...

I used to believe that the next book would be *the* book. You know, the one that would finally fix me. I've read hundreds of self-help books. Trauma books. Spirituality books. Inner child books. Productivity books. Each time I bought a new one, I felt hopeful. Maybe this author knows the secret sauce I've been missing.

But eventually, I realised something sobering: I didn't have an information problem. I had an integration problem.

The truth was, nothing would change unless I actually did something. I didn't need another 300 pages of insight. I needed to close the book, put down the highlighter and take action—even if that action was messy or small.

Self-help can be a beautiful tool, but it can also become a

hiding place. An intellectual cocoon where we feel like we're doing the work without ever touching the deeper layers.

It wasn't until I started applying what I'd read with tiny steps–awkwardly and imperfectly–that real healing began. And funnily enough, it didn't feel like a big breakthrough. It felt like making my bed. Drinking water. Going for a walk when I wanted to doom scroll. Healing started in the moments I stopped seeking the perfect method and started showing up for myself.

So if you're someone with a teetering pile of unread self-help books, this is your permission slip: You don't need to finish them all. You just need to *begin* taking action.

30

BECOMING MY OWN BEST FRIEND, PARENT AND HEALER

For so long, I believed someone else had to save me. I longed for deep, understanding friendships. Ones that would fill the ache I couldn't quite name. I clung to the idea that if someone really saw me, I would finally feel whole.

But here's what I've come to realise: The connection I was seeking outside of me was the one I needed to cultivate within. I had to become the one who saw me. The one who stayed. The one who said: *"You're okay. You're doing your best. And I'm right here."*

I used to spiral when someone didn't reply to a message:

"Why haven't they texted back?"

"Did I do something wrong?"

"Are they pulling away?"

Now, a softer voice steps in, one I had to build from scratch. This is the voice of my inner best friend, a part of me I wasn't even aware existed at first.

"Sweetheart, it's okay. People are busy. You're not being abandoned, you're just feeling tender. Let's take care of that feeling together."

This voice doesn't shame me for needing connection. It simply reminds me that I can honour those needs from the inside out. I don't need to abandon myself in order to belong. I can love and be loved, without losing myself in the process.

Journal Prompts: *Becoming the One Who Stays*

Take a quiet moment. Breathe. Then ask yourself:

- In what moments do I still search for someone else to fix, save or complete me?
- What would it feel like to be the one who stays—with compassion, softness and strength?
- How can I begin meeting my own emotional needs—not by denying others, but by honouring myself first?

Try writing a letter from your future self—one who knows how to hold themselves through anything. Let them remind you of how far you've come and how worthy you've always been of your own care.

The Drama Triangle

Developed by Stephen Karpman, the Drama Triangle is a model that describes a dysfunctional pattern of interaction where individuals unconsciously rotate between three roles:

- **Victim** – Feels powerless, seeks sympathy, avoids responsibility. (*"Poor me."*)
- **Rescuer** – Solves problems for others—often at personal cost. (*"Let me fix it."*)
- **Persecutor** – Critical, controlling, blaming. (*"It's your fault."*)

I lived most of my life bouncing between *victim* and *rescuer*. I rarely took the *persecutor* role—my low self-worth made me a magnet for others who did. People-pleasing was my superpower—and my prison.

A Personal Story: Rescuing at My Own Expense

A colleague once asked me if they could borrow money. I didn't have it to give, but I went to the bank, took out a cash advance on my credit card and handed it over anyway.

That one moment revealed so much: My inability to say no. My desperate need to be liked. My compulsion to rescue, even when I was drowning myself.

This wasn't compassion. It was codependency. I wasn't empowering her to find a solution. I was trying to save her. And in doing so, I betrayed myself.

Becoming My Own Best Friend

Then one day, it hit me: What if the best friend I'd been searching for was... me? Who knows *me* better than I do? Who's going to be with me for every single moment of my life? Who sees every version of me? Raw. Joyful. Broken. Rising.

Me.

This wasn't about giving up on friendships. It was about reclaiming the role of my inner best friend—the part of me that could offer comfort, encouragement and warmth. The one who whispers, "You've got this," when the inner critic is shouting.

Journal Prompts: *Becoming Your Own Best Friend*

- Am I treating myself with the same kindness I offer to others?
- How do I speak to myself when I make a mistake?
- Is my diary full of tasks, but no time for me?
- Am I expecting others to meet needs I haven't even acknowledged for myself?

Journal Prompt

Dear Me, I know you're doing your best. Here's what I want you to know today...

My Inner Critic Had a Megaphone

- "You're a waste of space."
- "Who are you to write a book?"
- "Don't even try."

If a friend spoke to me like that, I'd walk away. But this wasn't a friend, it was me. Or rather, a part of me: my inner critic. She had grown loud from years of shame and survival. Her job had always been to protect me—from failure, rejection, humiliation. She meant well. But her methods hurt.

And then, slowly, another voice rose up—the inner best friend, again.

"Of course you can write a book. Just go into a library—look at all those authors. You belong here too. You've got this."

Becoming My Own Parent

Parenting myself wasn't something I even knew I could do. I thought, *that ship has sailed*. But then I realised, I'm not a child anymore. I'm not dependent on my caregivers. I can become the parent I needed.

Before my first talk, I was terrified:

"What if no one comes?"

"Who do you think you are, calling yourself a speaker?"

But my inner parent stepped in with calm and steadiness:

"Let go of outcomes. Let go of numbers. Show up for yourself and your message. Your daughters are watching you model courage. That's enough."

During that talk, I invited the audience to dance to Staying Alive. Some joined in. Some watched. Both were perfect. I wasn't just teaching confidence; I was living it. And my inner parent was right there beside me, steady and proud, saying:

"You're doing brave things. I'm so proud of you."

The Inner Critic vs. Compassionate Voice

For a long time, I asked myself: *Am I doing this to myself?*

The spiral of shame. The self-doubt. The exhaustion.

And the answer? Yes… and no.

Yes. I believed the voice that said I wasn't enough.

No. Because that voice wasn't really me. It was an old recording. A protection strategy I hadn't realised I could pause.

Now, my compassionate self speaks more often. She sounds like a blend of my inner parent and inner best friend —kind but clear, loving but honest.

You're doing amazing.
Look how far you've come.
Keep going.

Understanding the Inner Critic

Your inner critic might echo the voices of

- A parent's harsh words
- A bully's insults
- A teacher's disapproval
- A culture that said you weren't enough

But that voice? It's not the truth. It's just old programming.

Name it. Talk back to it. Or gently thank it for trying to protect you and then make your own choice.

The Mantra That Carries Me

Holding my mala beads, I repeat:
I am loved
I am safe
I am free
I am abundant
I am enough
With each bead, I come back to truth—to calm, to myself.

Healing Practices

Inner Circle Visualisation

Draw a circle.
Inside it, write the voices you want close: Inner Parent, Inner Best Friend, Compassionate Self.
Outside the circle, place the critic, outdated beliefs and voices that no longer serve you.
Who gets to stay? You decide.

Journal Prompts

- What would my inner best friend say right now?
- If I were parenting myself with love today, what would I do differently?
- How can I soothe the critic instead of fighting her?

Final Thoughts

I used to think healing would come when someone else finally saw me, rescued me, chose me, loved me.
 Now I know:
 I am the love I've been waiting for.
 I am the parent I needed.
 I am the best friend I craved.
 I am my own healer.
 And the most beautiful part? So are you.

31

A JOURNEY INTO THE UNKNOWN—
MY AYAHUASCA EXPERIENCE

"Remember who you are," the ancient medicine whispered through my consciousness. It was exactly what I had forgotten after decades of carrying other people's shame. As I lay there in the dimly lit teepee, surrounded by the gentle sounds of rain and ceremonial music, I realised I was finally ready to reclaim my truth.

But let me start at the start of this transformation...

I had heard a lot about psychedelic healing for trauma and initially met it with intense resistance. The word "drugs" carried heavy baggage from my past. How could taking substances possibly help when I'd spent years trying to stay clean? It took months of research and soul-searching to realise that intention changes everything. This wasn't about escaping—it was about coming home to myself.

Journal Prompts

- What resistances are you holding about your own healing journey?
- What beliefs might be keeping you from exploring new paths to wholeness?

My journey to healing began at the British Psychedelic Society's sharing circles. Every six weeks, people gathered to talk about their experiences with sacred medicines. What struck me most was the purity of their intention. These weren't people seeking to numb their pain but rather to face it head-on; to understand and release it. Their stories planted seeds of possibility in my mind.

The question remained—where to go? The underground scene in the UK felt too risky. I needed structure, safety and expertise. That's when I met Sarah at one of the circles. She told me about a centre in the Netherlands that had been doing this work for over a decade. When I visited their website, something resonated deep within my soul; a felt sense that this was my path to healing.

In the months leading up to the retreat, nature began calling to me more insistently than ever before. Long walks became my daily ritual, as if my body already knew what medicine it needed. Even the dreaded winter darkness felt different this year. I dutifully used my SAD (Seasonal Affective Disorder) lamp, but I also found myself drawn to the quiet wisdom of the short days.

The dietary preparations became a ceremony in themselves. Giving up coffee was its own kind of awakening. After the initial headaches subsided, I discovered a new clarity in herbal teas. My body was already teaching me about surrender and transformation.

Understanding Ritual Preparation

Sacred ceremonies often require physical preparation. This isn't just about following rules, it's about creating space in your body and life for transformation to occur.

Entering the Darkness

The darkness of a London winter morning wrapped around me as I began my physical journey to transformation. The night bus at 3:38 AM carried me through empty streets, past the ghosts of my younger self—that girl who once rode these same routes home from clubs, full of artificial courage and numbed pain. How fitting that this journey toward healing would begin in darkness, just as my trauma once had.

The retreat centre emerged from the Dutch countryside like a dream—peaceful and welcoming, surrounded by woodland and green fields beneath December skies. The universe had gifted me a private room overlooking the serene landscape, a sacred space for the inner work ahead.

Three facilitators would guide our group of seven: Diana, the young Dutch woman whose gentle presence had welcomed me at the station; Michal, a tall Polish man with knowing eyes; and Shurandy, our lead guide, whose South American heritage seemed to bridge worlds.

As five o'clock approached, we gathered in the teepee. The space held us like a womb—warm, dark and full of possibility. The air was thick with the sweet smoke of sage and copal, ancient purifiers preparing us for revelation. Seven mattresses formed a circle around an altar at the front adorned with crystals, feathers and a lotus-shaped candle holder.

When the medicine first touched my lips, its bitterness shocked me—thick, earthy and ancient. This was not a substance for pleasure; this was plant wisdom in liquid form, demanding respect.

The Medicine Speaks

Sometimes the most powerful healing comes wrapped in bitter packages. *What difficult truths might you need to swallow to find your freedom?*

The first hour passed in profound silence as we each settled into our private journeys. Then, like watercolours bleeding into paper, the visions began. But instead of the darkness I had feared, the medicine took me somewhere unexpected—back to the light of my twenties.

Niki and Michelle appeared in my mind's eye, their faces bright with youth and possibility. We were at a Pulp concert, bodies moving to the music, hearts full of joy. A profound message washed over me:

"Stop being so hard on yourself for your past—you had so much fun. It was a life well lived."

The revelation hit me like a wave: I had been so focused on my trauma that I'd buried the joy. In trying to make sense of my pain, I'd written off entire chapters of my life as "wasted time." But the medicine showed me a deeper truth—even in our darkest stories, light finds ways to shine through.

Healing Insight

Trauma can act as a dark lens, colouring all our memories.
   Part of healing is reclaiming the light that always existed alongside the shadow.

Returning to Childhood

The journey then carried me back to childhood, but not to the scenes of abuse that had dominated my narrative for so long. Instead, I found myself at the family dinner table, surrounded by unexpected laughter. The greenhouse where the 'All Sorts Gang' held their secret meetings. The park behind our house where we played detectives, armed with little notebooks and boundless imagination.

   These memories weren't just escapes from pain—they were *proof* of my resilience–my capacity for joy even in difficult circumstances. The medicine was teaching me about the complexity of human experience, how light and shadow dance together in every life.

   A song played through the ceremonial space, reminding me that life is wonderful and horrible and short—a profound teaching about acceptance. All my years of trying to "get over" my trauma and here was the medicine showing me a different way—not to overcome, but to embrace the full spectrum of human experience.

Wisdom Teaching

Healing doesn't mean erasing the dark parts of our story. It means learning to hold both the light and the shadow, understanding that both are part of our wholeness.

Forgiveness Ladder

As the sun struggled to pierce the Dutch clouds the next morning, I felt drawn to the surrounding woods. Walking among the bare trees, a new intention crystallised: soul retrieval. I had recently encountered this concept—the idea that trauma can cause us to lose pieces of ourselves, fragments of soul that scatter in the winds of pain. Could I find these lost pieces? Could I become whole again?

I carried three objects into the second ceremony: a picture of little Daniela, my journal and a heart-shaped squishy toy borrowed from my daughter. Each item felt like a talisman, connecting past and present, pain and healing, lost and found.

The medicine revealed what I came to understand as the Forgiveness Ladder—each rung representing a deeper level of healing. At the bottom were the everyday resentments that had cramped my spirit. But as I climbed higher, I faced the profound betrayals that had shaped my life.

First Rung: The Stepfather

For the first time, I saw beyond my stepfather's actions to his own wounded soul. Generational trauma stretched behind him like a dark river—men who never had the chance to heal, who carried their pain forward in terrible ways. This wasn't about excusing the inexcusable, but about freeing myself from the weight of hatred.

Second Rung: The Father Who Left

My biological father appeared next—the man who had left me to my fate while parenting my half-siblings. The medicine showed me how holding onto this abandonment was abandoning myself. "Forgive him too and be free," it whispered.

Third Rung: The Mother's Knowledge

The most devastating revelation came next, hitting me with physical force: "My mum knew." The truth I had spent decades avoiding crashed through my defences. In our tiny house, how could she not have known? Yet simultaneously, I felt her devastation—a woman who had married a pedophile, whose own trauma response was to freeze, to deny, to survive.

The Paradox of Forgiveness

True forgiveness doesn't mean denying the wrongness of actions.

It means releasing ourselves from the prison of resentment while holding space for the complex humanity of all involved.

Tears streamed down my face as I wrote frantically in my journal: "So sad, it is all so sad." This wasn't the angry crying of before but a deep grieving for everyone caught in this web of pain—including myself.

Ripples of Healing

As the medicine continued its work, it revealed a truth both simple and profound: healing ripples outward. Each person I forgave created space for understanding someone else's pain. The facilitator's simple words—"So is mine," in response to my crying about my "messed up family"—illuminated this perfectly. We are *all* caught in these webs of intergenerational pain, all seeking ways to break the cycles.

Universal Truth

When we heal ourselves, we help heal the collective wounds that run through families, communities and generations.

The journey then took me to a specific memory: standing in the school annex, broken glasses in hand, terrified of going home. But this time, I wasn't alone. Adult me could be there for little Daniela, holding space for her fear and confusion. As I hugged her photograph, I made a sacred vow:

"I am so sorry you were so alone. I am here for you now and I will be the parent that you deserve. You will have everything you never had—love, encouragement and so much compassion."

The medicine showed me how Catholic messages of unworthiness had seeped into my young psyche: "Lord, I am not worthy to receive you..." But now, a new truth emerged: "Sweetheart, you are worthy. Mother Aya, I am saying the word—please help me to heal."

The medicine wasn't finished with its lessons in forgiveness. It brought forward Helen, my childhood friend. The message was clear: no resentment is too small to release, no hurt too minor to heal.

Like stones I'd been carrying in a heavy backpack, each person I forgave lightened my load:

- The investigator who didn't stand up for justice
- The teachers who didn't see my pain
- The friends who didn't understand
- And finally, hardest of all, myself

Songs filled the ceremonial space, lyrics carrying messages—a call to remembrance, a gentle urging to reconnect with the sacredness of life. The medicine had shown me exactly why I had come—not just to this ceremony, but to this life. Each challenge, each wound, each betrayal had shaped me, but they did not define me. I was here to reclaim my joy, to remember my worth and to learn forgiveness not as an idea, but as something lived and embodied.

Sacred Remembrance

Healing isn't about becoming someone new—it's about remembering who we've always been beneath the layers of pain and protection.

Integration of Forgiveness

The sun rose on a new chapter of my life. The medicine had shown me that forgiveness isn't a destination but a practice—not a one-time choice, but a moment-by-moment commitment to freedom. The tears, the laughter, the insights—they were all part of remembering who I am:

> A survivor who never lost her capacity for joy.
> A wounded child who grew into a compassionate adult.
> A sacred being having a human experience.

The message was clear: forgiveness wasn't just a nice idea or a therapeutic goal—it was a visceral necessity for my freedom. The medicine helped me realise just how much I had been carrying and showed me a path to finally set down these burdens, not through logical understanding but through deeply felt emotional release.

For those reading these words and recognising their own pain, their own need for forgiveness, I offer this truth: your life, too, is sacred. Your wounds can become wisdom. Your pain can become a purpose. And most importantly, you are worthy of remembering who you truly are—beneath the shame, beneath the trauma, beneath all the stories others have written onto your soul.

Journey Practice

> Take a moment now to place your hand on your heart and whisper to yourself:
> *I remember who I am.*
> *I remember why I came here.*
> *I remember my life is sacred.*

The medicine taught me that healing isn't about erasing the past—it's about integrating it into a larger story of transformation. Every tear shed in that teepee was a drop of relief in an ocean of release. Every insight was a step on the ladder of forgiveness. Every moment of remembering who I am was a return to the sacred truth that lives in all of us.

And perhaps that's the greatest gift of the medicine—not the visions or the insights, but the profound remembrance of our own sacredness, waiting patiently beneath the layers of forgiveness to be rediscovered.

As the ceremony drew to a close, I remained in the teepee, still clutching the photograph of little Daniela. The profound weight of the experience settled around me like a warm blanket. I had promised never to leave her alone again and this time, I knew I would keep that promise.

Later that evening, as we gathered for a nourishing bowl of homemade tomato soup, the group's energy shifted to lightness. They laughed about my tissue-throwing and light-waving during the ceremony—moments when I had been so deep in my process that I'd forgotten anyone else was there. A German lady who had been next to me spoke words that touched my heart deeply: "I really saw you in that moment," she said. She had truly witnessed the deep anguish I was processing.

Rituals and Realisations

The next morning, nature offered another gift for healing. At precisely 10:01 a.m., the full moon would reach its peak in the Netherlands sky. Drawn to the woods, I found myself creating an impromptu ritual—one my former self would have dismissed with an eye roll. But the medicine had shifted something fundamental in my approach to the sacred.

Two pinecones, found mysteriously stuck together, became powerful symbols of the two men who had shaped my life—my biological father and my stepfather. Under the full moon's witness, I offered a prayer that rose from depths I hadn't known existed:

"These two pinecones, bound together, symbolise two men who have shaped my life. My biological dad who gave me life and my stepfather who adopted me. To both of you I am now willing to truly forgive..."

Insight for the Reader

Sometimes the most powerful rituals are the ones that arise spontaneously, guided by the wisdom of our healing hearts.

The final ceremony was the San Pedro ceremony—gentler, more reflective. In this space, Mother Ayahuasca's teachings began to crystallise into practical wisdom. My journal captured the essence: "Amongst all the abuse was joy. There was joy, there was fun and there was laughter."

As if to underscore this truth, the ceremony's final song was Madonna's *La Isla Bonita*—an unexpected shift from the traditional ceremonial music that had filled our days. The song made me laugh. In the words of Madonna, "I fell in love with San Pedro."

Our final evening together became a celebration of transformation. The ceremonial songs that had carried us through our journeys became anthems of joy as we sang together: "Remember why you came here, remember your life is sacred." Even Frank Sinatra's *My Way* found its place in our spontaneous disco, until Robbie Williams' *Angels* was cut short by a dying speaker—a divine hint that it was time for rest.

As we departed one by one the next day, I was the last to leave. Chatting with the guides who had held space for such profound transformation, I found myself saying with genuine surprise, "That was kind of fun." In those simple words lay a profound truth—that even in our deepest healing work, joy finds its way through.

Integration: The Critical Path After Psychedelic Experiences

Just as I learned that embracing sobriety wasn't the end of my healing journey but the beginning, I discovered that psychedelic experiences aren't magic solutions. The real work begins in the days, weeks and months that follow. Integration—the process of absorbing and applying what was revealed—is where true healing takes place.

I've seen people chase one powerful moment after another—without lasting change. The journey may reveal truth, but it's the daily steps that transform it into growth.

In the early days, everything can feel raw and disorienting—much like early recovery. Insights may fade unless we pause to integrate them. Some days, this means journaling to capture a fleeting moment of clarity. Other days, it's taking one small, imperfect step: a brave conversation, a mindful pause, letting go of a habit that no longer fits. Integration can feel awkward at first—but awkward is where real life begins again.

Finding community is essential. Whether it's a therapist, a support group, or a friend who simply gets it—we need spaces that honour our process without judgment or exaggeration. We need mirrors that reflect back our growth, even when we can't yet see it ourselves.

Some insights will take root quickly; others will unfold slowly, like seeds beneath the soil. Approach this part of your journey with the same self-compassion you offered yourself in recovery. Integration isn't about doing it alone—it's about weaving new truths into daily life, gently and intentionally.

You're not just processing an experience, you're becoming a new version of yourself. Let it unfold. Let it land. Let it change you—bit by bit, in your own time and in your own way.

A Return to the Light

The ceremonies didn't erase the past but they illuminated it in a new way. I saw my story not just as one of survival, but of sacred remembering. I had retrieved lost parts of myself, released generations of pain and reconnected with joy I thought was gone forever. And as I stepped out of that teepee into the crisp Dutch air, something had shifted. I was no longer walking in the dark—I was being guided by something brighter.

Rewriting the Story

In the weeks that followed, I noticed a deep stillness inside me. The medicine had cracked open something I didn't even realise I was still carrying—not just the memories, but the meaning I had wrapped around them.

For so long, I had lived inside the story of what happened to me—a story shaped by shame, abandonment, betrayal. And even though I'd done so much work, I hadn't yet questioned the narrator. Who was telling the story? And more importantly—who was it serving?

Sadness had become my anchor to the past. It felt familiar, even safe. But at some point, the sadness wasn't just grief anymore—it had become identity. And I was tired of it defining me.

The medicine whispered that I didn't need to deny my pain in order to be free from it. I could honour the past without making a home there. I could carry the lessons—but not the weight.

That realisation—that I could write a new story, from the inside out—felt like liberation. A story where I wasn't a victim of my history, but the author of my healing. A story where my voice mattered more than my silence. A story where I could still hold the sadness, but with tenderness—not as my truth, but as one of many chapters.

So I picked up my pen—metaphorically and literally—and began again. Not to erase what happened, but to remember who I am.

Journal Prompts

Take a quiet moment. Breathe deeply. Bring to mind a chapter of your life that still feels heavy. Ask yourself:

- What story have I been telling about this part of my life?
- Is it still true—or is it simply familiar?
- What would a more compassionate version of this story sound like?
- What am I ready to let go of?
- What meaning am I ready to reclaim?

Journal Prompt

"If I were the author of my own healing story, this is how I'd write the next chapter…"

Let your heart lead. It doesn't have to be polished or perfect —just honest. Because you are not just what happened to you. You are what you choose to carry forward. You are the narrator now. And your story is still unfolding.

32

WHEN THE SOUL SPEAKS

There was one more layer of integration I hadn't expected, my relationship with the sacred.

When I was a child, God was a white man who watched in silence. He lived behind the altar, in stained-glass windows, in the voice of the priest who blessed us with holy water and gave us communion. God was everywhere, even in the priest's robes, they told me; and yet, He was nowhere when I needed Him most.

But in the silence of those unanswered prayers, a different kind of knowing began to stir—something older than dogma and deeper than ritual. Something I wouldn't fully reclaim until decades later, through brokenness, breathwork and finally, ayahuasca.

After the ceremony, as I began to integrate the visions and wisdom I'd received, I found myself circling one question again and again:

What does it mean to belong to the sacred, after the sacred has betrayed you?

The version of God I grew up with was rigid, conditional, toxic-masculine. He was echoed in the voice of the priest and in the shadow of my father. He punished. He judged. He turned away. When I was hurt, He did nothing. When I cried, I was told to pray harder.

That kind of God died the moment I truly decided to heal.

Ayahuasca cracked something open in me—a doorway to the divine that didn't require intermediaries. For the first time, I felt what it meant to be held, by something greater than myself, without fear. Not watched. Not tested. Just lovingly held.

I used to think I had to go through others to find God. But I've since learned to cut out the "middle-man."

I no longer need a priest to tell me whether I'm worthy. I no longer look to people behind pulpits or in collars to interpret the divine for me. I've lived the contradiction of trusting a man to lead me to God while he was hurting me behind closed doors. That kind of faith was built on fear. What I've built now is rooted in truth.

A pulpit is a raised platform where someone speaks on behalf of God. But I don't need someone standing above me anymore.

I don't need anyone to translate the sacred.

I've stepped down from that old hierarchy and into something far more intimate: a direct relationship with the divine.

After all the soul retrieval work, something shifted. It wasn't loud or dramatic but a quiet sense that my soul was back in the room with me. Awake. Present. And for the first time, I was truly aware of it.

And then something beautiful happened—unexpected, soft.

One morning during meditation, the words of a hymn drifted in. Words I hadn't heard in years, yet they landed with new meaning:

"*Here I am, Lord. Is it I, Lord?*
I have heard You calling in the night.
I will go, Lord, if You lead me.
I will hold Your people in my heart."

As a child, I had stolen a hymn book just to learn those words. I wanted so desperately to be chosen. To be useful. To be loved by the God I was told to fear. I didn't understand what those lyrics truly meant. I just wanted to belong.

Now, I understand.

It's not about being called to serve from a place of guilt or sacrifice. It's about rising from a place of truth. I don't need anyone's permission to speak. I don't need a collar, or a title, or a pulpit.

The sacred lives in me now. In my courage. In my voice. I hear the call, not from the platform of a church, but in the stillness of my own breath.

And this time, I answer from a place of peace: "*Here I am...*"

I no longer use the word "God" with the same certainty I once did. I use it with reverence now and caution. I know how easily that word can be twisted to control, to shame, to silence. But I also know that something sacred carried me through everything I didn't think I'd survive. Something gave me the courage to speak. To heal. To live.

Maybe it was God.

Maybe it was the part of me that remembered I am divine.

Either way, I've stopped trying to separate the two.

This wasn't a quick shift. I carried the scars of religious trauma deep in my body. For years, I thought God had abandoned me. That He didn't love me. That maybe He didn't even exist.

I don't need religion to access the sacred anymore. And that realisation has been profoundly liberating.

There are no rules now. No hierarchy. No robes. No shame. Just a quiet, unfolding relationship with mystery, with energy, with life.

I light candles not because I have to, but because it feels right.

I meditate not to prove I'm good, but to come home to myself.

I speak to something greater—not in desperation or pleading, but in trust and connection.

And when I do, I don't picture a bearded man in the sky. I picture light. Expansion. Warmth. I picture the version of me who never stopped believing there was more to life than just pain.

Because there is. There always was.

Healing my relationship with spirituality has meant redefining the word itself. For me, it's not about doctrines or answers. It's about connection—to breath, to earth, to others and to something ancient and alive that lives within me and around me.

It's the part of me that said, *not my shame.*

It's the voice that says, *keep going.*

It's the presence I feel when I teach yoga, when I cry, when I forgive.

I don't pretend to have it all figured out.

But I know this:

What hurt me was never the sacred.

What hurt me was the distortion of it.

And now I get to write a new story—one where I'm not just surviving trauma, but reclaiming my soul.

Journal Prompts

1. What messages about God or spirituality did you inherit in childhood?
2. In what ways did those messages support or harm you?
3. Do you still carry any beliefs that feel heavy, shameful, or fear-based?
4. When in your life have you felt most connected to something greater than yourself?
5. What would it feel like to explore a spiritual path that comes from within, not from external authority?
6. If you could talk directly to the divine, without any "middle-man", what would you say?

33

LIGHT : THE PATH TO HEALING

As I sat in quiet reflection, a song played softly in the background. Its melody settled over me, familiar yet stirring something deep inside. The words spoke of release, of letting go, of remembering the self that existed before the pain. I closed my eyes and murmured to myself:

"I am not my past. I am not my wounds. I am not the brokenness I once believed defined me."

Could I really be something more than my pain? Could I let go of the stories that had kept me trapped?

For twenty years, the same thoughts had circled in my mind like a storm:

"Why me? Why did this happen? It's so unfair. They destroyed me. I will never be whole."

I had every reason to cling to my suffering. After everything I had been through, how could I not? There had been so much darkness—could I find the light?

I did not have to keep carrying this pain. And so, the beginning of my **LIGHT framework** was born:

L – Let It Go
I – Integration
G – Grow
H – Heal
T – Time

Each of these steps became a guide to my healing.

Let It Go

One of the hardest lessons I had to learn was that letting go is not about erasing the past. It's about releasing its hold on me. For years, I carried my trauma like a heavy weight on my back. It shaped my identity, my relationships and the way I saw myself. I believed that holding onto my pain kept me safe, that if I let go, I would somehow be dishonouring my experience or letting my abusers "win."

But the truth is, holding on didn't protect me. It imprisoned me.

Letting Go Doesn't Mean Skipping Anger

One of the most surprising parts of my healing was realising how much anger I had stored. Not just at him, but at everyone who looked away. And at myself—for not speaking sooner, for not knowing better, for surviving instead of living. I had to learn that feeling angry wasn't a failure. It was a sign that my sense of justice had survived. Letting go didn't mean bypassing my rage. It meant giving it a voice, without letting it control the story.

Letting go isn't about forgetting or excusing. It's about releasing the past's hold on you.

It means choosing to no longer let the past define you. It means loosening the grip of suffering so you can finally breathe—so you can finally live.

Release the Story That Keeps You Stuck

We all tell ourselves stories about our past. Sometimes, those stories keep us trapped. For years, my story was:

"This pain will always define me."

"I will never be whole."

"They took something from me I can never get back."

But when I truly listened to the message of healing—that I had the power to rewrite my own narrative—I realised something: I could choose a different story for myself.

Instead of "They destroyed me," I whispered: "I am reclaiming myself."

Instead of "I will never be whole," I reminded myself: "Wholeness is my birthright."

Journal Prompts

What story about yourself are you ready to rewrite?

Sometimes, we don't even realise how much we are carrying: trauma, resentment, guilt, shame—all taking up space in our minds and bodies.

- What pain am I still carrying?
- What belief about myself is keeping me small?
- What part of my past am I afraid to release?

Write it down. Acknowledge it. You cannot let go of what you do not first bring into the light.

Practice Small Acts of Release

Letting go doesn't happen all at once. It happens in small, intentional steps:

- Breathing deeply and picturing yourself exhaling pain and inhaling peace
- Writing a letter to your past self—offering them forgiveness and love
- Saying out loud: "I release this weight. I am ready to be free"
- Moving your body walking, dancing, stretching to shake off emotional heaviness
- Creating a "letting go" ritual, like burning an old journal or tearing up words that no longer serve you

Accept That Letting Go Is a Process

It's not a one-time decision. It's a practice. Some days, the past will creep back in. That's okay. The goal isn't to never feel pain again, but to choose, again and again, not to live in it.

Each time you release even a little, you create space for something new: peace, joy and the lightness of being free.

Journal Prompt

> What is one healing practice you can commit to, even on the hard days?

Gratitude A Quiet Catalyst for Healing

In the middle of deep healing work, gratitude can feel almost too gentle to matter. How can we be grateful when we're grieving? What is there to thank when we're sitting in pain?

But gratitude isn't about denying what hurts. It's about making space for what's still good. It's about anchoring ourselves—however briefly—in what is working, what is beautiful, what is true.

When I started practicing gratitude, I didn't do it because I was feeling joyful. I did it because I was desperate for a shift—some way to not drown in everything I was feeling. So I began with the smallest things:

- I'm grateful for a warm bath.

- I'm grateful for my cozy bed.
- I'm grateful I got through today.

And it helped. Not in a performative, forced-positivity kind of way—but in a quiet, stabilising way. It reminded me that even while healing, I could still notice beauty. That joy and sorrow could coexist. That the present moment could offer tiny comforts, even when the past still ached.

Gratitude didn't replace my pain. It held it. It softened it. It reminded me I was still here.

Try This:

- Start or end your day by listing three things you're grateful for. They can be big or small.
- Try writing a thank-you letter to someone who showed you kindness—even if you never send it.
- Sit quietly and let your heart name one thing it appreciates right now. Just one. That's enough.

Gratitude won't erase the hard days. But it will create glimmers of peace within them.

Integration

At first, the "I" in LIGHT stood for "It's Not Your Fault." That message is still true. For years, I carried guilt, wondering why I hadn't spoken up sooner, why I hadn't protected myself. I needed to hear, over and over, "It was never your fault."

But as I continued to heal, I realised that knowing it wasn't my fault wasn't enough—I had to integrate all parts of myself. I had to stop rejecting my past and instead bring my wounded self back into wholeness. That's when I knew the "I" stood for Integration.

Healing isn't just about understanding what happened—it's about bringing all parts of yourself back together. For so long, I felt fragmented, as if my past, my pain and my present self were separate people:

- The child who suffered in silence
- The young woman who numbed the pain with alcohol, weed and distractions
- The adult me who was trying to heal but still carried the weight of the past

Through my healing work—especially Internal Family Systems (IFS)—I realised these parts of me weren't my enemies. They were protecting me the only way they knew how. I had to stop rejecting these parts of myself and instead invite them back home.

Speaking to My Inner Child

One of the most powerful moments in my healing was sitting in meditation and finally speaking to the part of me that had held all the pain.

I told her, "You don't have to carry this alone anymore."

I thanked her for protecting me and let her know that we were safe now.

For the first time, I was beginning to feel whole again.

Journal Prompt

How can you acknowledge and embrace all parts of yourself today?

Grow

Healing requires growth. And growth means change. For so long, I numbed myself with alcohol, weed and distractions. But when I stepped away from those habits, I had space—to learn, to rebuild, to grow into someone new. I:

- Trained as a life coach and founded Spiritual Survivors
- Learnt about trauma and healing
- Read books that expanded my perspective
- Started caring for myself in ways I never had before

We can't erase the past, but we can *choose* what we do with the present.

Journal Prompt

What is one small way you can choose growth today?

Heal

I made a promise to myself:
"I will do everything I can to heal."
For me, healing meant:

- Yoga
- Meditation
- Exercise
- Setting boundaries
- Facing my trauma head-on

Some days I still struggled. But I kept choosing healing, over and over.

Journal Prompt

What is one healing practice you can commit to, even on the hard days?

Time

Time does not erase trauma. But time—when used intentionally—can bring:

- Acceptance
- Self-compassion
- Peace

I used to think time was the enemy. That I had lost too many years. But time became my friend when I learned to use it for growth, healing and rediscovering my light.

In time, I found my voice.

In time, I wrote a book.

In time, I became LIGHT.

And in time, I allowed myself to grieve.

Not just the grief of what happened, but of what never did. The grief of the mother I had to walk away from, even though she was still alive. The grief of letting go of the hope that one day she might show up differently. The grief of the years I spent numbing myself with alcohol, years I can never get back, years I could have spent living, not just surviving. The grief of a childhood I didn't get to have, the innocence, the safety, the freedom to just be a child.

Grief became part of my healing. And it took time.

There were moments I wanted to rush through it, to tidy it up, to get to the "light" part faster. But grief doesn't work like that. It asked me to stay. To sit in the ache. To breathe through the heaviness. And slowly, it softened. It stopped screaming and started whispering.

Grief became a companion, not an enemy. A sacred space where I could honour all that had been lost and in doing so make space for all that was still to come.

Journal Prompt

> If you could send a message to your future self five years from now, what would it be?

Final Thoughts on LIGHT

This journey has not been easy. But I am here.

I let go of what was weighing me down.

I accepted that it was never my fault and learned to integrate my parts.

I grew into someone stronger.

I healed in ways I never thought possible.

I gave myself the time I needed to truly become light.

And if I can do it, so can you.

What will you do today to step into your own light?

As I moved through the light, into healing, wholeness and deep self-compassion, I began to understand something else. Healing isn't just about rising; it's also about returning. To the places we've avoided. The emotions we've buried. The parts of ourselves we've labeled unworthy or too much.

Because true wholeness isn't found by bypassing the dark, it's found by learning to sit with it, to listen and to welcome it home. And so, just as the light had illuminated so much, it eventually cast shadows too. It was time to meet them.

34

MEETING OUR SHADOW: THE PATH TO WHOLENESS

"Until you make the unconscious conscious, it will direct your life and you will call it fate." –Carl Jung

For years, I carried my pain in silence, not just the trauma itself, but all the emotions that came with it: the rage I wasn't allowed to express, the grief I pushed down, the shame that felt like a weight I carried, unseen but ever present. I tried to be good, to be quiet, to be what I thought everyone wanted me to be. I put one foot in front of the other, numbed myself, pretended I was fine. But deep down, a part of me was screaming to be seen.

That part was my shadow; the hidden, rejected and unprocessed aspects of myself I had buried to survive. At first, I thought healing meant getting rid of my pain, washing away the dark parts of myself so I could be pure, whole and light. But what I didn't realise is that healing isn't about getting rid of anything; it's about integrating, facing the parts of ourselves we've abandoned and learning to hold them with love.

There's a part of us that lives in darkness, not because it's evil or bad, but because somewhere along the way, we learnt it wasn't safe to let it see the light. For those of us who survived childhood trauma, this shadow grew larger with each moment we had to hide our pain, swallow our anger, or pretend we were "fine" just to survive.

You could liken the shadow to a room in your house that you've kept locked for years. Behind that door lives everything you couldn't express: the screams that stayed in your throat, the tears you couldn't shed, the rage and most painfully the shame that was never yours to carry. But here's what might surprise you: in that same room are also your untapped strengths, your wisdom and your remarkable resilience.

My psyche created these shadows to protect little Daniela when I was small and vulnerable, when hiding parts of myself was the only way to survive in my unsafe world. But we're not those helpless children anymore. The very fact that you're reading these words means you're ready to meet yourself—*all of yourself*—with new eyes.

When trauma shapes our early years, our shadow doesn't just quietly hide; it creates survival patterns that stay with us into adulthood. You might recognise its footsteps in the reflexive "yes" when you want to say "no," the automatic apology for taking up space, or the mysterious sabotage of opportunities just as things start going well. These aren't character flaws or personal failings—they're echoes of the strategies that once kept you safe.

People Pleasing & Fawning

I spent years believing I was just a "nice person". I was the one who said yes when I wanted to say no, the one who anticipated everyone else's needs before my own, the one who avoided conflict like my life depended on it, because at one point, it did.

What I didn't realise was that this wasn't just kindness. It was fawning, a trauma response where a person tries to appease or please others to avoid conflict, rejection or harm. Fawning is just as much a survival mechanism as fight, flight or freeze. Instead of running away or shutting down, we make ourselves agreeable, helpful and non-threatening in order to stay safe.

Signs of Fawning:

- Struggling to set boundaries because you don't want to upset others
- Feeling overwhelming anxiety when someone is mad at you
- Apologising excessively even for things that aren't your fault
- Feeling like your self worth is tied to being "useful" or "helpful"

The Golden Shadow

While we often think of the shadow as only the dark parts of ourselves, there's another side to it: the Golden Shadow, the light we refuse to own. This happens when we admire or even idolise someone, not realising that what we see in them is actually a reflection of our own potential. We project our unclaimed strengths, our power, leadership, creativity or confidence onto others instead of integrating them into ourselves.

How the Golden Shadow Shows Up:

- Hero Worship: Admiring someone so intensely that we feel we could never reach their level
- Envy: Feeling resentful of someone's success because deep down, we wish we could embody that too
- Self Doubt: Dismissing our abilities by believing we're not "ready" or "worthy" yet

For years, I admired people who were bold, confident and unapologetically themselves. I saw them as special, as if they had something I could never access. It took me a long time to realise the reason I admired them so much was because they were mirroring something inside of *me*—a part of myself I had yet to embrace.

Journal Prompts: *The Golden Shadow*

- Who do you admire most in life?
- What qualities do they have that inspire you?
- How can you cultivate those same qualities in yourself?

Healing Exercises: Meeting Your Shadow with Compassion

The Shadow Mirror: How are you triggered by others?

When someone's behaviour triggers strong emotions in you, they're often reflecting parts of yourself you've rejected.

Ask yourself:

- What qualities in others trigger you most?
- Do you suppress these same qualities in yourself?
- What did you learn about expressing these traits in childhood?

Healing Exercise: Writing a Letter from Your Shadow Self

Set aside quiet time to give voice to your shadow.

Begin with: *"I have been hiding because..."*

Let your shadow express its anger, grief or fear without judgment.

Then ask:

- *What does this part of me need?*
- *How can I show it compassion?*

Reparenting the Shadow: Speaking to Your Inner Child

Find a childhood photo or visualise your younger self.

Speak to them with the gentleness they deserved.

Say: *"I see you. I believe you. You are safe now."*

Write them a letter of love and reassurance.

The Light Within the Shadow

This journey isn't about banishing your shadows; it's about understanding them. It's about recognising that your shadow holds both wounds and gifts: the Dark Shadow of unprocessed pain and the Golden Shadow of unclaimed power.

For so long, I thought healing was about getting rid of my darkness. Now I know the truth: healing is about embracing *all of me*.

35

BECOMING LIGHT

This book hasn't just been about telling my story—it's been about surviving, remembering, breaking, rebuilding, and becoming.

Before I close this book, I want to thank my former self.

Thank you for not giving up. For walking into those counselling rooms. For sitting with the pain instead of running from it. For taking out the thorn that had been infecting your soul, even when it hurt like hell. For doing the deep, messy, sacred inner work—again and again.

There were times I wanted to give up and stay stuck in the story of being a victim. After all, I was a victim. It felt justified.

But here's what I've learned: what happened to me wasn't my fault. But healing? That's mine to claim. And that's a power no one can take away.

Returning to the Light

When I began writing, I didn't know how it would end. I didn't know if I'd find the right words—or the right courage. But I did know this: shame thrives in silence. And I wasn't going to stay silent anymore.

I used to think the darkness would swallow me whole. But I've discovered that even a flicker of truth, a breath of compassion, a moment of stillness can shift everything. The darkness still whispers sometimes. But I no longer fear it.

I've learned to turn towards the light—not to deny the pain, but to honour all the parts of me, even the ones I once buried.

To You, the Reader

Wherever you are in your journey—just beginning, deep in the process, or circling back—I want to speak to you directly.

To the one just starting to remember:

- Go gently. Take your time.
- You're not imagining things.
- Your body remembers what your mind tried to forget.

*To the one **deep in it:***

- You are not too much.
- You are not broken.
- Every breath you take is courage in motion.

∽

*To the one **who's been healing for years:***

- You're allowed to rest.
- You've done so much already.
- Healing isn't a race—it's a relationship with yourself.

∽

Wherever you are:
You belong. You are not alone.

What Healing Can Look Like

I won't pretend healing is easy. Some days I still get triggered. Some nights, tears come without warning. But now, I have tools. I have language. I have boundaries. I have breath. And most importantly: I have me.

I no longer run from the pain. I walk beside it. And that is what freedom feels like.

I've rediscovered joy, play, and possibility. I laugh more. I speak the truth. I honour what I need. I hold my inner child close. And I no longer confuse surviving with living.

A Gentle Practice

Before you close this book, pause. Take a breath. Place your hand on your heart. And say, with softness:

- "This was never my shame."
- "I am safe now."
- "I am becoming who I was always meant to be."

Or simply sit in silence and honour your strength. Let this be a threshold—not an ending, but a continuation.

A Closing Ritual

When you're ready, write a letter to the part of you that carried the shame—the part that stayed quiet, the part that survived. Say thank you.

Then release it in whatever way feels right: burn it, bury it, tear it up, or simply let it go.

You might choose to light a candle, whisper your name with tenderness, and say: *I am still here. I am still becoming. And I am free to write a new story.*

Keep going.
You are not your shame.
You are your courage.

～

YOU ARE NOT BROKEN, you are becoming. You are not what was done to you, you are who you choose to become—again and again.

Healing isn't about erasing the past. It's about reclaiming yourself from the ruins of silence, fear, and shame, and choosing to build something whole, something that is yours.

There is no finish line. Healing is a daily practice: nourishing your body, tending to your mind, and offering compassion when you slip—and you will.

There is no magic bullet. Only presence. Only return.

And the more you return to yourself, the more you'll remember: you are already worthy. You always were.

～

Final Words

You've reached the end of these pages—but not the end of your journey. This is the beginning of something new. A sacred, messy, beautiful becoming.

I'm so proud of you. Keep going.

The world needs your light. And more importantly—you need it, too.

Welcome home.

To your body. To your story. To yourself.

Remember:
> *You are worthy of healing.*
> *You are worthy of joy.*
> *You are worthy of freedom.*
> ***This is not the end.***
> ***This is your beginning.***

APPENDIX

Interview with EMDR Therapist

Daniela: Thank you so much for being here, Lucy. For the readers of my book *Not My Shame*, I think your perspective as both a therapist and a survivor will resonate deeply. Let's start with this: What inspired you to become a therapist?

Lucy: Thank you, Daniela. It's an honour to be part of this project. My journey to becoming a therapist was deeply personal. As a survivor of childhood trauma, I experienced firsthand how isolating and overwhelming it can feel. The concept of the "wounded healer" really resonates with me. I took the pain and experiences of my past and transformed them into a source of empathy and understanding to support others. There was a moment when I realised how profound it was to simply be heard, to have someone truly listen without judgement. That moment stayed with me and shaped my desire to provide the same kind of space for others.

The Wounded Healer

Daniela: That's so inspiring. I've heard the term "wounded healer" before. Could you elaborate on what that means to you?

Lucy: Absolutely. The term refers to someone who has gone through significant pain or trauma and uses that lived experience to help others heal. It doesn't necessarily have to be a therapist; it could be anyone offering support, guidance or compassion. What sets a wounded healer apart is the depth of understanding they bring. Having lived through the fear, shame and self-doubt that trauma brings, I can deeply empathise with my clients. But I also believe it's crucial to maintain boundaries and practise self-care. You can't pour from an empty cup. I also want to stress that being a wounded healer doesn't mean you have to be fully "healed" yourself. Healing is an ongoing process and part of the journey is learning alongside those you support.

Embracing Self-Care

Daniela: That's such an important point. Self-care can be challenging for survivors. What advice would you give someone struggling to prioritise themselves?

Lucy: Start small. One of the turning points in my own journey was when I realised it's okay to put myself first. I began setting small, achievable goals, like dedicating a week to doing things I genuinely enjoyed. It might feel unnatural at first, especially if you're used to putting others' needs above your own, but it's essential.

For me, affirmations like "I am worthy" and "I deserve peace" helped shift my mindset. Sometimes, self-care isn't glamorous. It can be as simple as saying no to something you don't have the energy for or setting boundaries with people who drain you. I also remind clients that self-care can look different for everyone. For some, it's a quiet walk; for others, it's dancing around their living room or taking five minutes to breathe deeply.

Practical Self-Care Tips

Daniela: Can you share more examples of self-care strategies that have worked for you or your clients?

Lucy: Certainly. In addition to affirmations, I encourage journaling, writing down your feelings or even crafting letters to your younger self. I've also found grounding exercises, like walking barefoot on grass or using sensory objects, to be incredibly helpful. For some clients, creating a "self-care menu" works well. This includes small activities, like lighting a candle, listening to a favourite song, or practising deep breathing.

The key is finding simple, soothing activities that bring comfort without overwhelming you. Another exercise I often suggest is visualisation, imagining a safe space, whether it's a real or imagined place, where you feel at peace. It can be empowering to create that mental refuge. I've even worked with clients to create physical safe spaces in their homes, a corner with comforting objects like blankets, photos, or scents that remind them of safety.

Addressing Shame

Daniela: Let's talk about shame, as it's a central theme in the book. What role does shame play in a survivor's healing journey?

Lucy: Shame is one of the most challenging emotions for survivors to navigate. It can keep you stuck, almost frozen and makes it difficult to reach out for help. For many, it's tied to anxious predictions, the fear of judgement or rejection if they share their story.

One of the most liberating realisations for me and for many clients I work with, is understanding that the shame does not belong to us. It was placed on us by the actions of others. Healing starts when we recognise that truth and begin to externalise the shame. I encourage survivors to challenge the internalised narratives that fuel shame. For instance, asking, "Whose voice is this? Is it mine or someone else's?" can be a powerful step toward reclaiming your sense of self. I also remind survivors that shame thrives in silence, so breaking that silence, even in small ways, is a significant act of defiance.

Overcoming Disclosure Fears

Daniela: That resonates so much. It took me 17 years to tell someone who wasn't in my family about my experience. How can survivors start that process of sharing when it feels so terrifying?

Lucy: It's completely normal to feel that way. If sharing feels overwhelming, start small. Write your thoughts down and then destroy the paper if you need to. Practise speaking to someone you don't know personally, like a helpline counsellor. Visualising a compassionate figure, someone who embodies non-judgement and safety, can also help.

Over time, building trust with a therapist or a trusted person can make it easier to take that first step. For many survivors, just saying, "This happened to me," out loud for the first time can be an incredibly powerful moment. It's also helpful to rehearse what you want to say. Practising in front of a mirror or writing down key points can ease the anxiety of sharing. I often remind my clients that courage isn't the absence of fear, it's feeling the fear and moving forward anyway.

Common Barriers to Disclosure

Daniela: You've shared so much wisdom about disclosure. Could you elaborate on some of the specific barriers survivors might face when considering disclosure?

Lucy: Absolutely. There are both physical and psychological barriers that survivors face.

Physical Barriers: Disclosure can impact living situations, especially if the abuser is a family member. Some survivors risk losing their housing or sense of security by speaking up. There's also the question of whether to report to the police, which is a major decision that shouldn't be taken lightly.

Psychological Barriers: Many survivors fear being disbelieved or having people question why they didn't physically resist. There's often intense shame and fear of judgement, with questions like "Why didn't you say something sooner?" Some survivors feel they owe their abuser something or that they're to blame for what happened. Others fear being viewed as mentally unstable.

Planning for Disclosure

Daniela: What advice would you give to someone considering disclosure?

Lucy: Planning is crucial. From my personal experience, I've learnt it's vital to carefully choose who you disclose to. Look for someone compassionate and stable who can maintain confidentiality if that's what you want. I made both planned and unplanned disclosures in my journey. While disclosing to my therapist was planned, I once shared my story with two aunts simultaneously. In hindsight, I would have preferred speaking to them separately.

Be prepared that disclosure can have ripple effects. In my case, living in a rural community, the information spread more widely than I intended, which led to social withdrawal. It's also important to understand that even well-meaning family members might not fully grasp the impact of trauma. I've had people say things like "Well, she looks okay now," not realising that high-functioning survivors can still be deeply affected.

Still in an Abusive Situation?

Daniela: What about survivors who are still in abusive situations? What should they consider?

Lucy: Physical safety must be the absolute priority. When I was at university, I was still being abused. He had such a powerful hold over me that I felt completely powerless to say no. Eight years of grooming and manipulation had left me utterly brainwashed. It's crucial to find someone trustworthy who can help you plan a safe way to end contact with the abuser, whether that's a family member or a professional.

This is where having the right therapist becomes invaluable. You need someone who can help you develop strategies and problem-solving skills. It's also important to note that during disclosure, survivors are particularly vulnerable. Some end up in abusive adult relationships that reinforce existing low self-worth. That's why connecting with support groups and professionals who can help safeguard you during the healing process is so essential.

Family Dynamics & Boundaries

Daniela: How about family dynamics? In my experience, responses can be very mixed. What's your take?

Lucy: Family estrangement or conflict is, unfortunately, very common among survivors. Trauma often doesn't begin with the survivor. It's intergenerational and families may lack the emotional tools or insight to respond supportively. This can lead to feelings of isolation.

That's why chosen families—building supportive, affirming relationships with people who align with your values—can be transformative. Surrounding yourself with those who validate and uplift you is a key part of healing. It's also helpful to set clear boundaries with family members who may be triggering or unsupportive. Setting boundaries is an act of self-preservation, not selfishness. I've worked with clients who felt guilty for setting boundaries, but over time, they realised it was one of the most loving things they could do for themselves. Boundaries aren't walls. They're bridges that allow healthier interactions to take place.

Therapy Approaches & Finding Purpose

Daniela: You've also mentioned therapy approaches like CBT and ACT. Could you explain how they help with trauma recovery?

Lucy: Certainly. Eye Movement Desensitisation and Reprocessing (EMDR) is an evidence-based therapy specifically effective for trauma. It helps you process distressing memories without needing to relive every detail verbally. For survivors, especially those dealing with shame or fear, EMDR can feel less overwhelming than other methods.

Cognitive Behavioural Therapy (CBT), particularly when combined with mindfulness-based approaches like Acceptance and Commitment Therapy (ACT) or Compassion-Focused Therapy (CFT), can also be invaluable. These therapies help survivors reframe negative thought patterns and build emotional resilience. One of my favourite exercises in ACT is focusing on *values-based living,* identifying what truly matters to you and taking small steps to live in alignment with those values.

Another tool I often use is the "thought record," where clients challenge distorted thoughts and replace them with more balanced perspectives. EMDR, on the other hand, helps untangle the emotional weight tied to traumatic memories, making them feel less overwhelming over time.

Envisioning a Better Future

Daniela: You've mentioned finding purpose in pain. Could you share more about how survivors can envision a better future?

Lucy: Many trauma survivors experience a foreshortened sense of future. They may feel like life will be cut short or that they won't survive past a certain age. I remember feeling as a teenager that I wouldn't live past 30. But this feeling, while common, isn't permanent. I encourage survivors to create vision boards of how they'd love their life to look in 10 to 15 years, even if it seems impossible from their current reality.

The gains from breaking your silence can be transformative. You get to stop toxic family patterns, create healthier relationships and reclaim your voice and sense of worth. Once I felt like everyone knew what happened, I paradoxically felt liberated. I no longer cared what others thought. I realised that what mattered most was that I knew the truth. This led me to reevaluate my life, let go of unhelpful relationships and choose friends who aligned with my values. Now I feel more accepted, loved and worthy than ever before.

Finding the Right Therapist

Daniela: For someone just starting therapy, what should they look for in a therapist?

Lucy: It's crucial to find someone who specialises in trauma and is registered with a professional body. If you're considering EMDR, ensure the therapist also has training in complementary approaches like CBT or clinical psychology. Most importantly, choose someone you feel comfortable with. Therapy is a partnership and trust is key. Don't be afraid to sample therapists until you find the right fit.

Remember, the right therapist won't just be skilled. They'll make you feel seen and heard. It's okay to ask questions about their approach and experience to ensure they're the right match for your needs. I also encourage survivors to listen to their intuition. If something feels off, it's okay to explore other options.

Lucy's Healing Journey & Barriers

Daniela: That's fantastic guidance. On a personal note, what practices have helped you most in your healing journey?

Lucy: Therapy has been central to my recovery, but I've also found immense value in meditation and spiritual growth. For me, exploring spiritual questions like "Why me?" led to a sense of purpose and peace. Meditation has helped me connect with my body and quiet my mind. I've also embraced the concept of leading my own life by setting boundaries and putting myself first. These changes have been life-changing.

Another practice I found powerful was writing letters—to my younger self, to my future self and even to people who hurt me (though I never sent them). Yoga and movement practices helped me reconnect with my body. Learning to celebrate small victories, like completing a yoga class or sitting with difficult emotions, was a key part of my journey.

Daniela: What do you find to be the biggest barriers to healing?

Lucy: Fear and shame are often the biggest obstacles. Survivors might worry about being judged or misunderstood. There's also the challenge of breaking patterns. Many survivors are so used to putting others first that prioritising themselves feels selfish. It's important to recognise that healing is not selfish. It's an act of reclaiming your life.

Another barrier is self-doubt. Survivors wonder, "Can I really heal?" The answer is yes, but it's a process requiring patience and self-compassion. A final barrier is the belief you have to do it all alone. Healing doesn't happen in isolation. Reaching out, even when it's scary, is vital. Unrealistic expectations can also hinder progress. Healing doesn't mean erasing the past. It means learning to live fully despite it.

Final Words of Encouragement

Daniela: Do you have any final words of encouragement for readers who may be struggling?

Lucy: Yes. Healing is possible. It's a journey that takes time, patience and immense courage. The first steps, whether it's sharing your story, seeking therapy, or even reading this book, are the hardest, but they're also the most important. Remember, you are not alone. There is a community of survivors and supporters who are living proof that life can be better—so much better—than it feels right now. Trust in your strength and know that you deserve peace and joy. Allow yourself to believe that brighter days are ahead. Healing isn't linear, but every step you take matters. You don't have to do it all at once. Just take it one day, one moment, at a time.

Daniela: Thank you, Lucy, for sharing your wisdom and vulnerability. I know your words will bring light and hope to so many.

Lucy: Thank you, Daniela. It's been a privilege to be part of this conversation and to have had you as a client. I hope it helps those who need it most.

A Note to the Reader

As you've read through this conversation with Lucy, I hope her words have brought you a sense of connection, understanding and encouragement. Healing from trauma is an incredibly personal journey and there's no "one size fits all" approach. It's okay to take your time, to start small and to find what works best for you.

Remember, as Lucy so beautifully shared, you don't have to face this alone. There is strength in reaching out, in sharing your truth with someone you trust and in finding a community of support. Every small step you take toward healing is a courageous act of self-love.

If you're unsure where to begin, try reflecting on the journal prompts included here. They are designed to help you explore your story, challenge feelings of shame and envision a future where you feel safe and valued. These moments of reflection, however brief, are acts of reclaiming your voice and your worth.

Above all, know this: you are not defined by what happened to you. You are so much more—strong, worthy and deserving of peace and joy. Healing may not be linear, but every step forward is a step toward reclaiming the life you deserve.

Take your time, be kind to yourself and trust that brighter days are ahead.

Exploring Your Story

- What would you like to say to your younger self who lived through the trauma?
- If sharing your story feels safe, what's one thing you might want someone to know about your experience?
- Write about a moment when you felt truly heard or validated. What did that feel like?

Processing Shame

- What messages about shame have you carried from your past? Whose voice do those messages belong to?
- Imagine placing the shame you feel outside of yourself. What does it look like? How would it feel to let it go?

- What's one thing you'd like to remind yourself about your worth, regardless of what you've been through?

Building Resilience

- What is one small thing you can do today to show yourself care and compassion?
- Think about a time you overcame something difficult. What strengths helped you through it?
- Write about a person, place or activity that makes you feel safe. What specific qualities make it comforting?

Envisioning the Future

- What would you like to say to your younger self who lived through the trauma?
- If sharing your story feels safe, what's one thing you might want someone to know about your experience?
- Write about a moment when you felt truly heard or validated. What did that feel like?

Boundaries and Relationships

- Who in your life feels like a safe and supportive person? How do they show you care or respect?

- What boundaries would you like to set in your life to feel more secure or at peace?
- •If you could create your ideal "chosen family," what qualities would those people have?

Self-Care and Healing

1. What is one activity, no matter how small, that brings you a sense of comfort or joy?
2. If self-care feels difficult, what's one belief or fear that might be holding you back? How can you challenge it?
3. Make a "self-care menu" of soothing activities. Include at least five things you could turn to when you need support.

Reflection and Growth

1. What does "healing" mean to you? How has that definition changed over time?
2. What's one piece of advice or wisdom from Lucy's interview that resonates with you most? How can you apply it in your life?
3. Write a gratitude list that focuses on moments of progress, no matter how small.

Want to Go Deeper?

If this book has resonated with your story and you're ready to take the next step in your healing journey, I offer personalised one-to-one coaching through *Spiritual Survivors*—my coaching practice for those ready to reclaim their voice, self and worth.

To explore coaching or book a free discovery call, you can reach me here:

- https://calendly.com/danielatilbrook/coaching
- danielatilbrook@gmail.com
- @danielatilbrook

Printed in Dunstable, United Kingdom